# MOVING IN THE SPIRIT

*also by Richard J. Hauser, S.J.*
*published by Paulist Press*

IN HIS SPIRIT

# MOVING IN THE SPIRIT

*Becoming a Contemplative in Action*

Richard J. Hauser, S.J.

PAULIST PRESS • New York/Mahwah

Library of Congress Cataloging-in-Publication Data

Hauser, Richard J.
    Moving in the spirit.

    Bibliography: p.
        1. Spiritual life—Catholic authors.     I. Title.
BX2350.65.H38       1986       248.4'82       86-2429
ISBN 0-8091-2790-3 (pbk.)

Published by Paulist Press
997 Macarthur Boulevard
Mahwah, New Jersey 07430

Printed and bound in the
United States of America

# CONTENTS

*To Mary Jo
my sister
teacher
and inspiration*

# INTRODUCTION

Years ago as a Jesuit novice I was taught that the goal of Jesuit spirituality was to become a contemplative in action. Even then I understood that contemplatives were special people, people who had achieved a very close union with God. I learned that there were two types of contemplatives: ones who sought a close union with God primarily by fidelity to personal prayer, others who sought close union with God primarily by fidelity to serving God's people. The religious orders up to the time of St. Ignatius, the founder of the Society of Jesus, had sought to help their members become contemplatives through prayer. St. Ignatius had a new vision: he hoped that his members would achieve an equally high union with God not primarily through prayer but through service to God's people. The goal he presented to his followers was to become contemplatives in action. As a follower of St. Ignatius this then was also my goal, and early in the novitiate I resolved to become one of these.

For many years I had a very inadequate understanding of how to become a contemplative in action. As I look back now, I can see that I was confused on three fundamental attitudes regarding Christian spirituality. First, I was confused most especially on the relationship between my personal efforts toward holiness and the role of God's grace. I saw becoming a contemplative in action as being totally in my own hands, completely dependent on my efforts. I did not understand the role of God in these efforts. I saw God merely as the rewarder of whatever good I accomplished by my efforts: the harder I tried, the more I pleased God, and consequently the more grace I earned. Second, this misunderstanding of the role of God in my spiritual life was compounded by a fundamental misunderstanding of human nature. I viewed human nature as basically untrustworthy if not actually evil due to original sin. Logically, then, I had to direct my efforts toward controlling or repressing the evil

1

tendencies that were part of this nature. I felt my growth in union with God would occur to the extent that I denied the basic thrust of my deepest self. Third, I had a very inadequate understanding of the method to become more closely united with God. I felt that growing in union with God demanded that I spend large amounts of time in explicitly spiritual activities such as liturgy, devotions, examination of conscience, and personal prayer. I had no adequate understanding of the importance of service to others as a means of growing in union. In short, during my early years as a Jesuit becoming a contemplative in action implied striving as hard as I could by my own efforts to please God, repressing my sinful nature and spending as much time as possible in explicitly spiritual activities. The result of my efforts brought little peace and much frustration. Headaches, even migraine headaches, were frequent occurrences during a typical week.

Fortunately my understanding of how to become a contemplative in action has shifted from these early years in the Jesuits. My three fundamental misunderstandings of the spiritual life have been radically changed. I now know that all growth in union with God flows from the Holy Spirit; my efforts, therefore, ought to be focused on responding to the Spirit. I also know that my human nature is fundamentally trustworthy because redeemed by Christ and that the grace of Christ in me is stronger than sin in me. Finally, I know that the cutting edge of my growth in union with Christ flows from the generosity of my service to others day by day and not from the length of time I spend in explicitly spiritual activities.

I believe that God has worked in me to transform my attitudes through three sources of inspiration. My primary inspiration has been the thought of Thomas Merton. My doctoral dissertation compared Merton's approach to religious experience with that of the psychologist Abraham Maslow. Through Merton is not directly quoted in this book, his insights were seminal in my renewed understanding of spirituality. He remains today the most influential spiritual writer in my thought. My second source of inspiration is a deeper appreciation of the role of the Holy Spirit in Christian life. Soon after leaving doctoral studies I began teaching courses on the Holy Spirit; I understood for the first time the necessity of the Spirit in all good actions. In addition I was struck by the compatibility of the theology of the Holy Spirit with the approach to spirituality of Thomas Merton. I recently published a book developing these insights: *In His Spirit: A Guide to Today's Spirituality*.[1] This book spells out in greater detail the presuppositions from Merton and from the theology of the Holy Spirit that I have taken for granted in this present book.

My third source of inspiration is a deeper understanding of the spirituality of St. Ignatius, focused especially on his Guidelines for the Discernment of Spirits and Method for Finding God's Will as found in the *Spiritual Exercises of St. Ignatius*.[2] This book was set in motion by the application of the theology of the Holy Spirit to Ignatius' guidelines for recognizing good and evil spirits in our lives. I began teaching a course on recognizing the Holy Spirit in daily life flowing from these insights. In addition I have been greatly blessed in recent years by exposure both in person and in writing to the foremost Jesuit exponents of Ignatius' thought on discernment of spirits and finding God's will: George Aschenbrenner, Michael Buckley, Avery Dulles, John English, John Futrell, Thomas Green, Karl Rahner and Jules Toner.[3] I am especially grateful to Frs. Aschenbrenner and Toner. It was a series of lectures from Fr. Aschenbrenner during the summer of 1974 which initially began my thinking on the discernment of spirits in daily life and a course from Fr. Toner in the summer of 1983 that gave me the insight into Ignatius' full thought on the discernment of spirits.[4] Every page of my book reflects the thinking of some of these Jesuit scholars.

Not too long ago I heard myself telling a group of students how to become a contemplative in action. I was struck by the audacity of my own statement and questioned myself: Do I really have a method to teach others? I answered affirmatively. I afterward understood what I had taught them was largely a result of the three sources that had influenced me the most in recent years. But I also saw that what I said was definitely not simply a commentary on St. Ignatius' Guidelines for the Discernment of Spirits and Method for Finding God's Will nor an expansion of one of the authors I admired. It was a personal synthesis taken from many sources to which I had been exposed in recent years. This book, then, is a very personal approach to becoming a contemplative in action with no one to blame but myself—hopefully under the inspiration of the Spirit.

The book moves rather simply. The first three chapters are closely related. Chapter 1 discusses the experience of Christians as they are awakened for the first time to the movement of the Spirit within their own heart. Chapter 2 gives the criteria for recognizing these movements of the Spirit in daily life. Chapter 3 presents a practical method for recognizing and handling inner movements that do not flow from the presence of the Spirit. Chapter 4 switches directions slightly and discusses a method for seeking God's will for significant decisions by reflecting on our inner experiences. Chapter 5 concludes the book by presenting a method for keeping a spiritual journal directed toward recording the presence and absence of the Spirit in our day.

I have included reflection questions at the end of each chapter. These questions are key to grasping the chapter; they are directed at relating the matter to our own personal experience. The cutting edge in understanding and growing in spirituality is not simply learning new ideas; it is applying these ideas to our own experience to see whether they make sense. Only if they do should they be taken seriously. I suggest the following process for getting the most out of these chapters: first, read the chapter slowly and reflectively; second, answer the reflection questions in terms of your own experience; third, decide what you want to integrate into your daily life; fourth, share your answer with others. It may be necessary to discuss the ideas in the chapter in order to understand them well enough to apply them to your own experience. This discussion should never, however, take the place of relating the ideas to personal experience.

Finally, the title of the book is significant. My basic insight is simple: we become contemplatives in action to the exact extent that we move in the Holy Spirit. This book presents goals that may at first seem overwhelming and unreachable. But it really presents nothing that Christ hasn't already asked. For Christ's goals for us *are* overwhelming. Christ asks us to love and serve God and our neighbor with our entire heart, soul, mind and body. And indeed these goals are overwhelming and unreachable—without the Holy Spirit! The contemplative in action is one who has learned the "trick" of recognizing the Holy Spirit in inner experiences and allowing the Spirit to move his or her heart toward Christ's goals step by step, day by day. The contemplative does not worry about reaching the goal by some future deadline; the contemplative is too concerned with living and loving now. For the contemplative it's not the "getting there" that is important but the "moving in the Spirit." This book presents some practical techniques to use day by day for moving in the Spirit with the conviction that becoming a contemplative in action is in God's hands and so there is no need for us to worry.

# I AWAKENING TO THE HOLY SPIRIT

There is a very important moment in our journey toward union with Christ; it is a moment that deserves much more attention than it is usually given by spiritual writers. It is called the awakening or the awakening of self to the Spirit within our experience. The awakening is a watershed in following Christ. Before the awakening a conscientious Christian attempts to follow Christ by responding faithfully to external laws and to the teaching and example of Jesus. After the awakening the Christian attempts not merely to live life in conformity with the external laws and teaching of Jesus but to respond to the internal direction of the Holy Spirit within experience. Most books about spirituality presume that the reader has been awakened to the presence of the Spirit within the self. This book also begins with that presumption. However, since the topic is generally not discussed in much detail, it seems good to describe exactly what we mean by the awakening and to put it in the context of the entire Christian spiritual path. Before doing this, however, I will present my understanding of the goal of Christian spirituality and then present key aspects from the scriptural view of the person that are essential for understanding this book adequately.

## Spirituality as Responding to the Spirit

Each of us is led by God toward an understanding of Christian spirituality that best meets the needs of our temperament and life situation. I believe it is helpful to articulate our own approach so that we can apply it explicitly to every area of our lives. I have been led by the Lord to understand the goal of Christian spirituality as my effort with God's grace to respond always to the movement of the Spirit within myself.

We know that the completion of Jesus' work for our salvation occurred on Pentecost with the sending of the Holy Spirit to the Christian community. We know too that the Spirit has dwelt within the community throughout the years and abides in it today. The Holy Spirit is the animating force both of the community's life together and of the life of each individual member of the community. The Spirit is, simply, our sanctifier. St. Paul put the matter as simply as it could be put: "Since the Spirit is our life, let us be directed by the Spirit" (Gal 5:25).[1]

This particular approach to Christian spirituality has been very helpful for me in meeting my personal needs. Like many of us, I have an inferiority complex. This tendency causes me anxiety in my relationship with God. In order to feel good about myself I must be "perfect" before God. This means that I must execute exactly all the prescriptions of God and the Church. This tendency toward perfectionism was aggravated when I entered the Jesuit order. During my early years in the Jesuits there was a great emphasis placed on the complete observance of all the rules of the order. I was told as a young Jesuit that the goal of our life was to obey God's will and that was expressed to us through the rules of the order and the commands of the superior, even the smallest ones. I, therefore, made it my goal to observe all these rules and commands. I was frequently anxious because I often failed in this observance; I felt God was displeased.

As I grew as a Jesuit, I became aware that I had a rather shallow notion of serving God. I became aware that my efforts ought not to be focused simply on the external conformity of my actions to the rules presented to me but on the internal quality of heart with which I performed my deeds. I gradually came to see that the external performance of good deeds was as good as the internal love with which they were motivated. Indeed, Jesus in the Gospel clearly taught his followers not simply to conform to the external law but rather to be faithful to the law of love that arose in their hearts. He himself frequently broke the external law. Consequently I gradually shifted the focus of my spiritual goals from the conscientious performance of external actions to a loving service of God and others in my actions. I simultaneously felt free to let go of certain external performances that did not seem to help my service to the Lord. As I did this I noted that my habitual mood was changing from less and less anxiety to more and more internal peace. I began to appreciate Paul's message in Corinthians: "Now this Lord is the Spirit, and where the

Spirit of the Lord is, there is freedom'' (2 Cor 3:17). For the last twenty years this idea has remained uppermost in my own Christian living and has enabled me to deal constructively with the perfectionistic tendencies of my temperament.

However I must emphasize that responding to the movement of the Spirit is a goal that is important to me because of my temperament and life situation. There are other equally valid ways of presenting the goals of Christian spirituality. Perhaps it is not an over-generalization to say that these goals fall within four approaches. Responding to the Spirit is one of the approaches. Another, and perhaps the most common, is imitating Jesus. Many Christians put the focus of their spiritual life on getting to know Christ through studying the Gospel and then imitating the example of Christ in their personal lives. Still another approach is centered on being faithful in doing God's will. Christians choosing this goal make every effort to discover what God is asking them to do and then spend their lives faithfully attempting to fulfill this will. This is the approach that Jesus himself presented in the prayer he taught his disciples: ''Thy Kingdom come, thy will be done.'' It seems also to be the focus of Jesus' own spiritual goals. Finally, an approach of many Christians is simply loving and serving others. These Christians concentrate their efforts on being faithful in helping other people, especially those who are most in need. Traditionally, then, the goals of Christian living have focused on responding to the Spirit, imitating Christ, doing God's will and serving others. Each approach is equally valid; each approach can be supported easily by plentiful references to the New Testament. But most importantly, each of the approaches complements the others. No single approach is valid unless it includes references to the others; the approaches are merely entry points for a personal internalization of the Christian Gospel. It is important that we choose the approach that best meets the needs of our temperament and life situation. The rest of the Gospel message will fall into place around this particular starting point.

Let me illustrate this using my own entry point. How does my approach complement the other three approaches? First, the Spirit is central in any imitation of Jesus: ''No one can say 'Jesus is Lord' unless he is under the influence of the Holy Spirit'' (1 Cor 12:3). The New Testament teaches that I cannot even recognize Jesus as Lord without the Spirit. In addition the Gospel teaches that the Spirit I have received is the same Spirit that moved Jesus: Jesus was conceived, baptized and led by the

Spirit throughout his entire life. Therefore the more I am open to this Spirit of Jesus the more I will become like Jesus, imitate Jesus. Second, the Spirit I have received is sent to me from the Father. It is the Spirit of the Father. Only because I have received the Spirit can I recognize God as my Father and truly live as a child willing to do my Father's will.

> The Spirit you received is not the Spirit of slaves bringing fear into your lives again; it is the Spirit of sons, and it makes us cry out, "Abba, Father!" The Spirit himself and our spirit bear united witness that we are children of God (Rom 8:15–16).

And third, the Spirit I have received is the Spirit of God and God is love. The primary effect of the Spirit in human life is love of God and love of neighbor. The more I am open to God in me, which is the same as saying to the Spirit in me, the more I will desire to love and serve my neighbor.

> My dear people, let us love one another since love comes from God and everyone who loves is begotten by God and knows God. Anyone who fails to love can never have known God, because God is love (1 Jn 4:7–8).

To the extent that I am open to the movement of the Spirit in me I will imitate Jesus, love and do the Father's will, and love and serve my neighbors.

It should be added that there are ways of expressing the goals of Christian spirituality that are not fully compatible with the message of the New Testament. We frequently hear people express these goals in language such as the following: avoid sin, keep the commandments, earn grace, get to heaven, save my soul. These goals, while good in themselves, are not adequate expressions of Christian spirituality because they are primarily self-centered. They put the focus of spirituality not on the Father, Jesus and others but on the self. All valid New Testament approaches to spirituality are other-centered, not self-centered. Jesus summarized it best in his statement of the two great commandments: "You must love the Lord your God with all your heart, with all your soul, all your strength, and with all your mind, and your neighbor as yourself" (Lk 10:27). It is almost taken for granted in the New Testament that if we seek to love and serve God and others there is no need to worry about avoiding sin, keeping the commandments, growing in grace and getting to heaven. All this happens spontaneously without self-conscious effort. As we respond to the Spirit and fall more and more in love with Jesus and the Father, we naturally try to avoid all those things that offend them and do all those things which please them. And it is unthinkable that Jesus and the Father will not take care of us in this life and also in the next.

## Self-Indulgence and the Holy Spirit

The approach to spirituality we are presenting presumes an acceptance of the scriptural view of the person. From the very beginning it must be acknowledged that Scripture presents us not only as having inner movements toward goodness flowing from the Holy Spirit but also as having inner movements away from goodness which do not flow from the Holy Spirit. The scriptural understanding of the person is complex, but it will be sufficient to summarize the teaching by emphasizing three major themes. These themes are presumed throughout this book. First, human beings are basically good and therefore the movements coming from our deepest center can be trusted. This theme is clear in both the Old and the New Testaments. There are two stories of our creation in the Old Testament, both of them highlighting the inherent goodness of our human nature. In the first story we are presented as being created in God's own image.

> God said, "Let us make man in our own image, in the likeness of ourselves; let them be masters of the fish of the sea, and the birds of the heavens, the cattle, all the wild beasts and all the reptiles that crawl upon the earth." God created man in the image of himself, in the image of God he created him, male and female he created them (Gen 1:26–27).

We recall that, having completed creation, God looked over the work of the six days, climaxed by the creation of man and woman, and "God saw all he had made, and indeed it was very good" (Gen 1:31). In the second Old Testament creation account this goodness is highlighted because we are presented as proceeding from the breath of Yahweh.

> Yahweh God fashioned man of dust from the soil. And he breathed
> into his nostrils a breath of life, and thus man became a living being
> (Gen 2:7).

We human beings are created by the very breath or Spirit of Yahweh and
we are created in Yahweh's image. The Old Testament writers could do
nothing more to show the inherent dignity of the human person.

As we have already seen, the New Testament also presents humans
as fundamentally good because of our redemption through the grace of
Jesus Christ. After Pentecost the believers in Jesus lived a new life, a
life flowing from God, the life of the Holy Spirit. And because they had
received the life of the Spirit they could now truly be called children of
God. Emphasizing the dignity of the human person because of the Spirit,
Paul uses another powerful image: "Your body, you know, is the temple
of the Holy Spirit, who is in you since you have received him from God"
(1 Cor 6:19). This passage was especially important for Paul's hearers
because the Jewish people had traditionally localized the presence of
God in their temple. Paul is telling them that if God's presence can be
localized anywhere it is within themselves. The conclusion of the Old
and the New Testament message on the human person is that we are good
through our creation and our redemption; therefore our innermost being
can be trusted.

The second theme present in both the Old and the New Testament
is that we humans also have within us inclinations away from good and
toward evil. It was clear to Paul that these inclinations did not come from
the Holy Spirit but from ourselves outside the Spirit, sometimes referred
to as the "flesh." Indeed in many passages of his writings Paul is graphic
in describing the inclination toward evil and self-indulgence that is present within ourselves when we do not operate under the influence of the
Holy Spirit. The following passage is Paul's classic statement of the tension within ourselves between the Spirit and self-indulgence.

> Let me put it like this: if you are guided by the Spirit you will be in
> no danger of yielding to self-indulgence, since self-indulgence is the
> opposite of the Spirit, the Spirit is totally against such a thing, and it
> is precisely because the two are so opposed that you do not always
> carry out your good intentions.
>
> When self-indulgence is at work the results are obvious: forni-
> cation, gross indecency and sexual irresponsibility; idolatry and sor-

cery; feuds and wranglings, jealousy, bad temper and quarrels; disagreements, factions, envy; drunkenness, orgies, and similar things. I warn you now, as I warned you before: those who behave like this will not enter into the kingdom of God.

What the Spirit brings is very different: love, joy, peace, patience, kindness, goodness, trustfulness, gentleness, and self-control (Gal 5:16–23).

Likewise in the clearest possible terms in the opening chapters of the Old Testament, the sinfulness of the human race is highlighted in the stories of Adam and Eve, Cain and Abel, Noah and the flood, and the tower of Babel. The intent of these stories is to show that evil in the world proceeds not from the creation of God but from the disobedience toward God by human beings. All these stories teach us that from the beginning we human beings yielded to inclinations from within ourselves to go against the word of God. Though God made us good, God also made us free. It is the abuse of our freedom that brings sin and evil in the world. It is the clear teaching of both the Old and the New Testament that not every inclination that arises within us can be trusted.

The third truth clearly taught by the New Testament regarding human beings is that Christ's death has freed us from the power of sin, and therefore we need no longer be dominated by sin. The New and Old Testaments teach that there are indeed all-pervasive influences toward sin arising within our being. But the New Testament also teaches that since we have been redeemed, the grace of Christ has saved us from being helpless before this power of sin. Even though we experience evil inclinations, we remain in the Holy Spirit; our deepest identity is still as children of God and temples of the Spirit. Because grace in us is stronger than sin in us, we can trust our deepest self. This is why the Gospel is such ''good news'' for Paul—and for us!

So then, my brothers, there is no necessity for us to obey our unspiritual selves or to live unspiritual lives. If you do live in that way, you are doomed to die; but if by the Spirit you put an end to the misdeeds of the body you will live (Rom 8:12–13).

## Awakening: From Law to Spirit

Paul teaches us that we Christians must ever be watchful of our inner motivations to see whether or not they flow from the Spirit. Paul also teaches another lesson related to the Spirit that is essential for growing in union with the Lord. He was talking to Jews who had been nourished on the Old Testament commandments. These people had attempted to direct their lives by the external written laws as presented in the Old Testament. Good as this was, Paul taught that this was not sufficient for a total following of Jesus. No external law could direct them toward imitating Christ completely; the only law they could use for a guidance in totally imitating Christ was the law of the Holy Spirit written on their hearts. It was this law, Paul taught, that had now replaced the old written law as their fundamental guide in the spiritual life.

> But now we are discharged from the law, dead to that which held us captive, so that we serve not under the old written code, but in the new life of the Spirit (Rom 7:6, New American Bible).

Paul saw this transition in his own life and in the life of his community as a new freedom: ". . . where the Spirit of the Lord is, there is freedom" (2 Cor 3:17). Paul seems to have experienced the obligations of the old law as something superimposed on himself and his community. In contrast to this he experienced the law of the Spirit of Jesus as something that spontaneously arose within himself and his community and was natural for human living because it flowed from their deepest selves. We often find Paul contrasting the written law with the law of the Spirit.

> This great confidence in God is ours, through Christ. It is not that we are entitled of ourselves to take credit for anything. Our sole credit is from God, who has made us qualified ministers of a new covenant, a covenant not of a written law but of spirit. The written law kills, but the Spirit gives life (2 Cor 3:4–6, New American Bible).

This awakening to the Spirit within ourselves as our primary guide in following Jesus is the key to all growth in Christian life. But before we reach this stage of imitating Christ, we all pass through the stage of following as faithfully as we can the teachings and the laws given us by Jesus and presented to us by our Church. Indeed our desire to observe these laws flows from the Holy Spirit within us. However as we grow in openness to the Lord, we find that the observance of these external criteria for following Christ are not sufficient. The focus of our morality is internalized and the action of the Spirit is intensified. Gradually we attempt to bring every area of our daily life under the influence of this law of the Spirit. Though our external actions may appear the same to observers, the internal motivation has radically changed; we are attempting to live our life in response to an internal movement and not simply in conformity with an external directive given to us. This is the new freedom of the children of God which we have seen Paul discuss. Only after we have experienced this awakening can we be truly said to be on the Christian spiritual path. Indeed, it is only after this awakening that we can speak of the goal of Christian spirituality as responding to the Spirit. Fidelity in responding to the Spirit will bring us into deeper and deeper union with Jesus and lead us to the highest union with God. The accompanying diagram presents the Christian's spiritual path in terms of our relationship with Jesus and the effect of this relationship on our daily living and our personal prayer.

### THE CHRISTIAN SPIRITUAL PATH

| Stages of the Journey | Focus of Daily Living | | Quality of Prayer |
|---|---|---|---|
| Unawakened Self | Law and Commandments | | Vocal |
| | (Relationship to Christ by fidelity to obligations) | | |
| | **AWAKENING OF THE SELF TO THE SPIRIT** (Relationship to Christ by fidelity to the Spirit) | | |
| Purgative Way | Imitation of Christ: Patterns of action | | Talking to the Lord |
| | Continuing conversion: Temptations | | Mind active |
| | | Fluctuations of heart | Meditation |
| | | Fluctuations of action | |
| Illuminative Way | Imitation of Christ: Quality of heart | | Being with the Lord |
| | Continuing conversion: Temptations | | Mind attentive: I-Thou |
| | | Fluctuation of heart | Beginning contemplation |
| | | No fluctuation of action | |
| Unitive Way | Imitation of Christ: Zeal for service | | Being one in the Lord |
| | Continuing conversion: Temptations | | Mind absorbed in Lord |
| | | No fluctuation of heart | Advanced contemplation |
| | | No fluctuation of action | |

The unawakened self does not know Jesus well. The relationship to Christ is defined primarily by the conventional norms presented by the Church for this relationship. The goal for daily living becomes fidelity to keeping the laws and commandments of the Church. Similarly the goal and reason for prayer of the unawakened self is fidelity to the obligations for prayer that the Church prescribes. This may include Mass on Sunday as well as daily meal prayers and night prayers. There may also be intense moments of prayer for deeply felt needs. For the unawakened self Jesus is an acquaintance rather than a friend. Since prayer is an expression of our relationship with Jesus and the relationship is not intense, prayer is not usually intense. Prayer is often understood as "saying one's prayers."

With the awakening everything changes. Jesus moves from an acquaintance to a personal friend. Sometimes this personally experienced relationship with Jesus is referred to as being "born again" or as a conversion. We are no longer faithful to the relationship with Jesus because it is a religious obligation; we are faithful because Jesus has become our friend. This affects our daily living. Our effort is not simply to keep the commandments that have been prescribed for us but to imitate Jesus completely and become more and more like Jesus in loving and serving God and others. This new relationship also affects the quality of our personal prayer. Since Jesus has become our friend, we now desire to express this relationship in a new, spontaneous form. We pray not because we "have to" but because we "want to."

Since this awakening is so central for our union with Christ, it is important to reflect on how this awakening occurs. I believe it occurs in two ways. For some it happens naturally with the passage from adolescence to young adulthood. During this time our reflective and emotional capacities develop. In addition we are becoming more and more independent and concerned with forming our own views on life and not having those views dictated by our family, society or religion. Especially if we have left home and are on our own, we may become concerned with finding a personally meaningful practice of our faith, a practice that responds to our own needs and not merely a practice that reflects our previous indoctrination. The young adult and college years can be an important time for this internalization, especially if there are people who encourage questioning and reflection on inherited religious beliefs. Many of us, then, find ourselves growing toward a practice of the Christian faith during this time that flows more from our own internal desire to know, love and serve Christ than it does from the need to conform to the dictates of our previous religious authorities.

For some, however, this awakening does not happen naturally with the passage from adolescence to young adulthood. It may be delayed to a much later time in life, and it may require a special and dramatic experience for its occurrence. There are very many types of occurrences that can precipitate an awakening. They may flow from very positive life experiences such as the following: a good retreat; an encounter with a convinced believer; a memorable sermon, movie or book; attendance at a stirring religious service. The awakening may also occur in an effort to cope with a very negative and life-threatening experience such as the following: break-up of a treasured relationship; career frustration and failure; accident, illness or death of a loved one; a theology course that challenges religious assumptions; conflict with parental or religious authority; coping with the problem of evil in the world and the existence of God.

I believe my own awakening happened during the second semester of my senior year of high school. I recall very vividly even today having a very different relationship to God after this semester than I did before. Before the second semester I was a conscientious, conventional Christian, even belonging to and being active in our high school sodality. My spirituality focused on avoiding sins, keeping the commandments, and performing regular religious duties such as Sunday Mass and monthly confession. I am not aware of having any deep relationship with Christ before that time, and I cannot recall setting time aside for personal prayer to develop a relationship, though I am aware of praying intensely for special favors at different times. By the end of the semester my entire relationship with Christ had changed. What I recall most vividly was the difference in my personal prayer. I found myself "sneaking up" to the parish church in the late afternoons and evenings and sitting in the dark in front of the Sacred Heart altar. I recall experiencing a deeper peace and joy in Christ's presence than I had ever known before. I can also remember getting up earlier to attend the Mass that was offered daily at my high school before classes started. And I also recall going to Perpetual Help devotions in our parish on Tuesday evenings. I was very embarrassed about praying so much and told no one about it. I had a new relationship with Christ, and I wanted to be with my friend.

As I reflect on this semester, the only event that might have occasioned this deepening was my confusion on what to do after graduation—to go on to college or to apply to the Jesuit novitiate. It was in the context of this new experience of Jesus that it began to make more sense to me to seek admission to the Jesuits than to go to college. I did not know anyone who prayed as much as I did. It seemed to me that only priests and sisters prayed in this way, so perhaps Christ was asking me to be a priest. However I believe that my awakening was   gradual one that came with my personal development in maturity, though perhaps it was precipitated to some degree by the question of what I wanted to do with my future life. From that point on everything changed in my relationship to Christ.

## The Spiritual Path: Continuing Conversion

If we are faithful to the guidance of the Spirit in our daily life, we can trust that the Spirit will lead us to the very highest levels of union with Christ and service to his people. In order to recognize the working of the Spirit in our own life, it is helpful to summarize the usual experience of people who have been awakened and are consistently trying to live their life in tune with the Spirit's guidance. The three stages through which people pass are usually called the purgative way, the illuminative way and the unitive way.[2] We will briefly discuss each of these stages in terms of their general relationship to Christ, the process of the continuing conversion and the quality of personal prayer.

The stage of the spiritual path experienced during and after the awakening is usually called the purgative way. How does the Holy Spirit affect our relationship to Christ in the purgative way? As we have seen, Christ is no longer simply an acquaintance about whom we have heard from others and know casually; Christ has now become our personal friend: the Spirit has awakened in us a deeper desire to know Christ, to love him and to serve him. We begin our imitation of Christ by rearranging the patterns of actions in our life to be more in accord with his actions. We must add patterns to enable us to better know Jesus. We find ourselves desiring to spend more time with him both by reading the Gospels and by talking over our own life with him. We simultaneously begin doing more things for other people, becoming increasingly uncomfortable with our self-centeredness.

It takes a while to bring our actions into conformity with Christ's; our continuing conversion in the purgative way occurs on the level of our external actions. I find it helpful to distinguish the conversion occurring in the three spiritual stages by comparing and contrasting experiences of temptation, the fluctuation of heart and the fluctuation of action. The awakening does not take away temptations. Indeed temptations will be with us for our entire life; Jesus was tempted. It should be stressed, however, that their presence or absence is no indication of personal holiness; how we deal with them is. The purgative way is the beginning of the spiritual journey. As can be expected, we experience many temptations. Having experienced these we find our hearts attracted toward the temptation and moving in the direction of infidelity to Christ. Since we are just beginners in the spiritual path we find our actions often yielding to these temptations. For instance I experience a temptation of jealousy toward a co-worker. I become aware of this and in my heart begin demeaning this person by whom I am threatened. Finally this attitude gets translated into action as I use the next opportunity to ''talk down'' this person to someone else. However in the purgative way we are not dealing with patterns of serious or mortal sin; our awakening to the Lord moves us to avoid serious sin. And we do have a general desire to be converted from all our sin. But this conversion comes only slowly as we are faithful in responding to the Spirit in the depth of our heart. We find that in some areas of our life we are doing quite well and the habits of sinfulness are receding, but in other areas we are not doing as well.

What, finally, is the quality of personal prayer in the purgative way? Since we have been awakened to a desire to know Christ better, we experience ourselves wanting to be with Jesus and to pray more; we are not content merely with saying the prescribed prayers expected of all Christians. But our efforts to pray in the purgative way are often difficult at the beginning because it is hard to quiet down; it may take great effort to concentrate. Since the focus of our prayer is to get to know Jesus so that we can better imitate him, prayer will be marked by much talking with the Lord, making resolutions to imitate him more closely and reviewing our life to see how well we are doing. In traditional terminology, the prayer of the purgative state is called discursive meditation if thinking about Jesus predominates, and it is called affective prayer if making acts of love and of the will predominate. In both experiences the mind is active under the influence of the Holy Spirit.

The next stage of the spiritual path is the illuminative way. What is the predominant quality of the imitation of Christ in this stage? To a great extent we have eliminated the external patterns at odds with Jesus' teaching and example, and we have substituted many positive rhythms allowing us to become more like Jesus. To the outside observer, in fact, our lives may appear completely sinless. Without a great deal of effort we find that our hearts are responding to the Spirit's presence in our daily actions and we are becoming more like Christ. The comparison with human friendship is helpful. The opening stages of getting to know a friend are often painful. We must yield patterns of selfishness in order to accommodate ourself to the other person. Having done this, however, we find a new level of communion arising. Our friend remains gentle on our mind; our hearts and actions move consistently and effortlessly toward our friend. The Spirit is now holding us toward Christ in a similar way. Because we are held toward Christ without a great deal of personal effort, we can be said to have entered the initial stages of becoming a contemplative in action. Our habitual union with Christ is flowing over and affecting all our actions without the same amount of effort it required when we were in the previous stage of the spiritual path.

And yet sinfulness remains and so the need for conversion. Since our external actions are for the most part in conformity with the example of Christ, we are now led by the Spirit to look more deeply at the quality of heart which underlies them. The focus of living at the illuminative stage is not only to imitate Christ in our external actions but also to imitate Christ's internal attitude of continually loving and serving the Father and others. It helps to understand this stage by comparing it with the experience of temptation, fluctuation of heart and fluctuation of action in the purgative stage. Like every human being we continue to experience temptations, and we often allow our heart to dwell on these selfish and self-indulgent attitudes. However there is a difference from the purgative stage. Since the Spirit has been mightily at work in us, the temptations usually do not flow into our actions. For instance we now experience a temptation to jealousy of a co-worker. We become aware of this temptation and may even be willing to indulge ourself by demeaning the person in our heart. However the temptation stops at this level and does not flow into our outward actions. The focus of our moral effort has shifted from external actions to our internal quality of heart. In the illuminative stage our effort is to become progressively more aware of the shifting quality of our heart so that we come to recognize automatically those internal movements that do not flow from the Spirit and so refuse to allow them to flow into actions. The approach to spirituality I am describing in this book is useful for all Christians who have been awakened to the presence of the Spirit. I believe, however, that it is most suited for those Christians who are now attempting to imitate Jesus within the illuminative way.

As may be expected, the quality of our prayer in the illuminative way also deepens. Since prayer is the expression of our relationship with the Lord, as our relationship grows so does our prayer. This relationship has come a long way since our awakening; Jesus has become our best friend. It is no longer necessary to do a lot of thinking to get to know him better. We are now drawn by the Holy Spirit to rest quietly in his presence with very little activity of our mind and will. As with human friendship we find ourselves simply enjoying being with our friend without the necessity of doing a lot of talking; we are attentive to the presence of our friend and enjoying an I-Thou relationship with him. There are, of course, times when we do become more active in our prayer, making an effort to get to know Jesus better in order to integrate Jesus' example more deeply into our own life. But in general, our prayer is marked by a quiet resting in the Lord. In the traditional terminology this quality of prayer is referred to as "beginning contemplation." The term *contemplation* implies that our own efforts to pray are decreasing and the activity of the Spirit in our prayer is increasing. Happily there is a relationship between contemplative prayer and being a contemplative in action. The same Holy Spirit that holds our heart to God in prayer also holds our heart toward serving others outside of prayer.

The final stage in the spiritual path is called the unitive way. St. Paul gives us insight into his experience of the Lord at this level of union: "I live now not with my own life but with the life of Christ who lives in me" (Gal 2:20). This is the life of perfect friendship with the Lord. Its dominant characteristic is an increased zeal to serve God in all that we do. Our previous efforts of service do not seem to be enough. The Holy Spirit has been at work purifying our hearts and actions, and we now find ourselves existing with the desire totally to serve the Lord and not being torn from this desire by selfish needs. Perhaps this level of union can be compared to a perfect human friendship occasionally found in married couples or good friends. After years of relationship with one another couples and friends may find that they are utterly sensitive to the other's needs and not held back by personal selfishness in being responsive to these needs. Their fulfillment comes in serving the other.

What are the characteristics of continuing conversion at this level of union? Like every human being we continue to experience temptation; Jesus experienced temptations. However these temptations do not hold our heart away from serving God nor do they flow into actions. As we become aware of the temptation, we dismiss it through the power of the Spirit and reaffirm our desire to serve the Lord. In short we handle the temptation the same way the Lord did: ''Be off, Satan! For Scripture says: 'You must worship the Lord your God, and serve him alone' '' (Mt 4:10). For instance, as soon as we become aware that we are experiencing a temptation to jealousy, we turn away from it, neither allowing ourselves to indulge in the selfish attitude nor letting the temptation affect our actions. In the unitive way, then, there is no deliberate sinfulness in actions or in thoughts. We may be caught off guard at times and not recognize a temptation toward sinfulness, but as soon as we do, we turn from it.

The quality of our prayer in this stage also deepens. The activity of the Spirit has increased to such a degree that we are held in union with the Lord with almost no use of our own faculties. In addition, we find that we are slipping into a union that is not mediated by self-consciousness. In the illuminative way we enjoyed a conscious attentiveness to the presence of God; in the unitive way we find ourselves slipping away from this conscious attentiveness, forgetting ourselves and being absorbed in oneness with God. It is similar to the experience of concentrating on something so totally that we are not even aware of the fact that we are concentrating until we emerge from the experience. This type of self-forgetfulness and absorption may be present in earlier stages of prayer, but it is not present with the same degree or frequency. This prayer is called ''advanced contemplation.'' There is a clear relationship between this contemplation and the zeal for serving God: the same Spirit that has transformed our service has now entirely taken over our prayer. Since the activity of the Spirit is at its greatest at this level of union, it is the person in this state that can be called most fully a "contemplative in action." It seems that very few of us live on this level of union habitually.

Here a brief clarification is in order. The spiritual path really has two meanings. The first is the successive states of the spiritual life that follow one another in our growth in union with God, that is, the purgative, illuminative and unitive ways. But the spiritual path also has a second meaning. It also refers to the complementary moments of purgation, illumination and union present within each period of growth in union with the Lord. For instance, beginners on the spiritual path may experience at times the deepest union with God in prayer; those well advanced may find themselves caught in an embarrassing pattern of sinfulness and so need a deep conversion in some aspect of their life. The path is more cyclic than linear. We have attempted to describe the dominant characteristics of each stage, realizing that we experience aspects of each stage all along the way. But it remains true that as we grow in union with the Lord, we find our experience marked more by the characteristics of one stage than of the others.

## Be Not Anxious

As a young Jesuit I worried much about my spiritual growth. I was concerned to get out of the purgative way as soon as possible and move into the illuminative way. I saw the project as being entirely in my own hands; if I did not become perfect, I had not put enough effort into it. My efforts were centered around conformity to rules, prayer, silence, reflection on my life. I was convinced I could earn union with God by these efforts. I now realize that much of my effort was misplaced; I placed the project of my spiritual growth in my hands and not in God's. I do realize that growth in union does not come automatically and does indeed require effort. But I now know that the focus of my effort must be living in tune with God in my daily life and so allowing God's Spirit to draw me to ever greater union and love. Happily, I no longer worry about the project of my spiritual growth: I have turned it over to the Lord. I know that this growth will come in God's time, not my own. Since we become contemplatives in action to the extent that we live in tune with the Spirit, it is now necessary to discuss the criteria for recognizing the Spirit within our inner experience.

## REFLECTION QUESTIONS

1. Describe your personal spiritual goal. Is this goal similar to or different from the four general approaches described in the chapter? From your starting point, how do you integrate the other approaches suggested in the chapter—imitating Christ, doing God's will, loving others, responding to the Spirit?

2. Reread Paul's quotes from Galatians 5:16–23 on self-indulgence and the Spirit. Using this criterion list activities of recent days that were not done under the influence of the Holy Spirit.

3. Describe your awakening. When did it happen? Was it gradual or sudden? Was it precipitated by any particular event in your life?

4. Looking over the patterns of your daily life, both prayer and action, which seem more reflective of the purgative stage?

5. Describe elements of the illuminative way you recognize in your prayer and action.

6. Are you aware of ever having experienced the absorption in God characteristic of prayer in the unitive way? Are you aware of patterns of zeal for service that are totally transformed by the Spirit because they seem to be unaffected by personal selfishness?

# II  RECOGNIZING THE HOLY SPIRIT

After we have been awakened to the presence of the Spirit, a new moment arises in our spiritual life. Our effort is now directed to responding to the internal law of the Spirit written in our heart rather than simply conforming to the external obligations as they have been presented to us by the authorities in our life. We do indeed continue to fulfill these obligations, but our reasons have been more deeply internalized. And responding to the Spirit is a far more challenging project. It demands that we habitually live in tune with our inner experiences, distinguishing those which flow from the Spirit from those that do not. The term "inner experience" will be used throughout this book; by it we simply mean all those movements that arise within ourselves, such as our memory, imagination, thinking, feeling, and willing. This chapter will discuss the criteria for recognizing the Holy Spirit within these experiences. Before doing this, however, it is necessary to reflect on the role of the Spirit in all good actions.

## The Necessity of the Spirit

From our earliest years of religious education we have learned that the Holy Spirit is our sanctifier: the Father creates us, the Son redeems us, and the Holy Spirit sanctifies us. We know that the Spirit is our sanctifier because the Spirit continues the work of Jesus. At the Last Supper Jesus told his disciples that it was necessary for him to leave them for a while. They were very sad at this. And Jesus then asserted, even more strongly, that he must go but that it was better for them that He did go.

> Yet you are sad at heart because I have told you this. Still, I must tell
> you the truth: it is for your own good that I am going because unless
> I go, the Advocate will not come to you; but if I do go, I will send
> him to you (Jn 16:6–7).

The Gospel tells us that it is God's plan that the Holy Spirit continue
Jesus' work and that only if Jesus leaves can the Spirit come. The Spirit
would now take Jesus' place as teacher, comforter and advocate with the
Father. And the Gospel insists that it is even better for them that Jesus
go because through the Spirit Jesus could be more intimately present to
them than he was during his earthly life. The Spirit is the culmination of
Jesus' work of redemption; it is only through the Spirit that we can be
led to Jesus and to the Father. The life of the entire Church as well as
the life of the individual Christian flows directly from the presence of
this Spirit. The following prayer taken from the Eastern Church presents
this truth beautifully.

> Without the Holy Spirit, God is distant,
>     Christ remains in the past,
>     the Gospel is a dead letter,
>     the Church is just an organization,
>     authority a domination,
>     mission is propaganda,
>     worship a ceremonial,
>     and Christian way of life a servitude.
>
> But in him: the cosmos is uplifted and groans
>     in giving birth to the kingdom,
>     the risen Christ is here,
>     the Gospel throbs with life,
>     the Church is communion in the Trinity,
>     authority is a liberating service,
>     mission a Pentecost,
>     the liturgy both memorial and anticipation,
>     and human life is deified.

We Christians accept the fact that the Spirit is our sanctifier without
questioning; however we do not usually avert to the fact that the Spirit
is absolutely necessary for every good deed. The role of the Spirit and
the necessity of grace for all good actions was one of the first truths to

be defined by the early Church. During the time that the early Christians were clarifying their understanding of God as Trinity and of Jesus as one person with two natures, they were simultaneously clarifying their understanding of the necessity of grace for every good action. This truth was clarified very early in the fifth century because it was challenged by a group in the Church generally referred to today as the Pelagians. These people believed that some good deeds could be performed by our own efforts without the need of the internal power of the Spirit sent by Jesus. Christ was important for them not because his work culminated in the new life of grace through the indwelling of the Spirit but because through his teaching and life he gave an example of how to live. The early Church quickly corrected this error: Christ saves us through the indwelling of the Spirit and not simply by providing an external model to be imitated. The first Christians saw very clearly that if the Pelagians were right, we would be saved not by the grace of Christ but by our own efforts.

Another group called today the semi-Pelagians then arose and in an even more subtle way attempted to undermine the centrality of the grace of Christ for salvation. They admitted that the Pelagians did not give enough role to this grace. They held that internal power from Christ was indeed necessary for the performance of good deeds. However they also held that this power was not operative until we humans had initiated the good desire on our own. After we had made the first move toward the good action, then the grace of Christ came into play to confirm this desire and give us the power to carry it out. The early Church saw that this modified version of Pelagianism was not true to the teaching of the New Testament. It put the initiative toward good actions primarily in our own hands since we took the first step by our own effort. The Church in responding to the semi-Pelagians insisted that the very first inner movement of our heart toward a good action flowed from our response to the grace of Christ and not from our own initiative. From the fifth century onward Christians have believed that the desire for good as well as the power to carry it out flows from the grace of Christ. St. Augustine led the Church in responding to those who were undermining this truth. This quote, taken from his response to the Pelagians, reflects the Church's traditional belief.

> Therefore, no one has true wisdom or true understanding, or is truly eminent in counsel and fortitude, or has either pious knowledge or

knowledgeable piety, or fears God with a chaste fear, unless he has received "the Spirit of wisdom and understanding, of counsel and fortitude, of knowledge and piety and fear of God" (Is 11:2–3).

No one has true power, sincere love, and religious sobriety, except through "the Spirit of power and love and sobriety" (2 Tim 1:7).

In the same way, without the Spirit of faith, no one will rightly believe, and without the Spirit of prayer, no one will profitably pray.[1]

The accompanying diagrams are very helpful in understanding the Church's teaching on the role of the Holy Spirit in all good actions. The scriptural model is clearly the model presented in Scripture and defended by St. Augustine. The intersecting areas of the triangles represent the presence of the Spirit in our inner movements toward good. As we grow in union with God, the area of intersection can be imagined as increasing. The area outside the intersection indicates the proportion of inner experience that habitually flows outside the influence of the Spirit. The goal of Christian spirituality is to allow all our inner experiences to fall under the influence of the Holy Spirit. Whether our stream of thoughts, images, feelings and desires arise spontaneously within ourselves or arise in reaction to external situations, we desire that the Holy Spirit direct these always toward greater love and service of God. Since the Spirit initiates all movement toward good within us, we can recognize the Spirit in all the experiences that point us toward good. Likewise we can recognize the absence of the Spirit in inner experiences that are pointing us away from the desire to love and serve God and others. We can call the indwelling of the Spirit in us by the traditional term of sanctifying grace; we can call all promptings toward good actions flowing from this indwelling by the traditional term of actual grace.

The Western or the Pelagian model is clearly at odds with Scripture, misunderstanding the origin of our inner desires and movements toward good. In this model all inner experiences moving toward the desire to love and serve God and others are seen to flow from ourselves apart from the grace of God within us. God's role is seen as rewarding us with grace for the good which we do on our own initiative. This grace is understood as increasing or decreasing according to our behavior. Since this grace is imagined as existing outside ourselves, it cannot be the origin of our good actions. Those of us living with this Western understanding of the self and God will never appreciate the all-pervasiveness of the presence

*Origin of Good Actions*

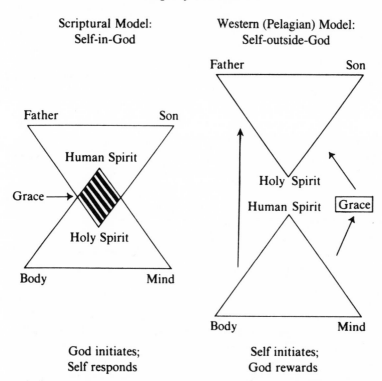

Scriptural Model:
Self-in-God

Western (Pelagian) Model:
Self-outside-God

God initiates;
Self responds

Self initiates;
God rewards

of grace in our life. Even the group called the semi-Pelagians are at odds with the Gospel. Although they do acknowledge the necessity of grace to confirm and carry out our good desires, they do not acknowledge that the initiative toward the good comes from the presence of grace. The Western model clearly distorts the fundamental message of the New Testament and the teaching of the Church since the fifth century. I am convinced that this is the most misunderstood aspect of Christian spirituality. Most of us simply take for granted this Western model: God is seen as totally outside ourselves and consequently as having no real effect on our inner desires toward good.

I recently discovered a very simple way of assessing the prevalence of the Western model in our understanding of spirituality. When we were young we were asked a basic catechism question: "Why did God make us?'' We were then given a very simple answer: ''God made us to know, love and serve him in this life and to be happy with him forever in heaven.'' Most of us have understood this definition from a self-outside-God model. We understood that if by our own effort we did everything we could to know, love and serve God we would then be rewarded by eternal life in heaven. We carried this basic misunderstanding of God's role into adulthood. I believe it characterizes much of our thinking on spirituality even today. It should quickly be added that God did make us ''to know, love and serve him in this life and be happy with Him forever in heaven.'' However it must be emphasized that God did not leave us unaided in fulfilling this purpose. Through the indwelling of the Spirit God is always drawing us toward deeper knowledge, love and service. Our role in the process has always been to be sensitive to these inner drawings and to respond faithfully to them.

Why does this Western model of spirituality have such a hold on us? First, I believe we are conditioned into this model without even consciously reflecting on it. From early childhood on we are rewarded and punished by significant persons in our life as our behavior deserves. Unreflectively we assume that God relates to us as these significant persons. Surely this is true for our relationships to our parents. As a child we are told that God is our Father. We automatically presume that God will reward or punish us for our deeds the same way that our mothers and fathers do. When we leave home and enter school, we find that our teachers are rewarding and punishing us according to the results of the work we do in school. As we grow into adulthood, we find employers acting the same way. Another reason for the all-pervasiveness of the Western model in our thinking is that this understanding of the relationship between God and ourself was formed when we were psychologically incapable of imagining God being within us. We assumed that the Father and Jesus exist as persons outside of ourself, and therefore we should relate to them as we do with human persons. We surely do want to insist on the transcendence of God—for God's existence is not simply co-extensive with human existence—but we want to emphasize equally the immanence of God. Unfortunately, most of us take our approach to God from childhood into adulthood with us. We don't bother to rethink our spirituality and ask whether God can, indeed, be present within us as well as exist outside of us.

Finally, I believe that this Western model is also reinforced by psychological theories of human motivation. The theories of motivation we study are complete in themselves and attribute all behavior to natural, psychological influences. We accept these psychological explanations for our behavior and never bother to ask whether some of our inner experiences could also be explained by the influence of the indwelling Spirit. Since we live in a secularistic society, it is usually presumed that all factors of human motivation will eventually lead to scientific insight by psychologists who are professionally engaged in this work. We neglect to look at the Gospel to see what insights on human motivation are present there.

Granted that God initiates all movements toward good in our life, what then is our role? Are we simply passive observers of God's action? Emphatically no! Our role is to become sensitive to these inner experiences in order to recognize when the Spirit is and is not present and then to follow only those experiences that are from the Spirit. The choice of whether or not to respond to the Spirit is always in our own hands. God draws us toward good; God does not force us to do good: our freedom remains central. The deliberate non-response to the movement of the Spirit within us is the most profound way to understand the meaning of sin. We Christians have always said that sin is an offense against God. Sin is directly against God because it is a free choice to move against the Spirit's lead. These choices often flow into our external action, becoming a violation of God's written commandment and frequently an offense against God's people. But the origin of sin is deep in our hearts in our free choice not to move in tune with the Spirit. The good deeds we perform under the influence of the Spirit are, then, our own deeds because we have freely chosen to perform them. However these good deeds, far from making us proud, ought to make us humble. We are humble because we recognize that the source of our goodness is ultimately God's indwelling; without this presence we are helpless to do any good thing. As we grow in this conviction, we grow in humility; as we acknowledge the greatness of the good we are doing, we simultaneously recognize its ultimate source. Our attitude becomes like the attitude of Mary who acknowledged her greatness but also acknowledged the source of that greatness: "My soul magnifies the Lord and my spirit rejoices in God my Savior because he who is mighty has done great things for me and holy is his name."

## Criteria for Recognizing the Holy Spirit

After we have acknowledged the necessity of the Spirit for all good deeds, the question arises, "What criteria can we use to recognize the Spirit within our experience?" We know it is not adequate to look at external actions to see whether the Spirit is active. We can perform externally good actions for very poor motives, and therefore not be under the influence of the Spirit. This is the problem that the New Testament has with the Pharisees. Our criteria for recognizing the presence of the Holy Spirit must then be directed at our inner experiences: our imagination, memory, feelings, intellect, will. The question then becomes, "Which of our inner experiences provide the best criteria for recognizing the presence of the Spirit?" I believe the most reliable criterion lies in the activities of our will, or, more precisely, in our desires. If our heart is moving toward the desire to love and serve God and others, the Spirit is present. If our heart is not moving toward that desire, the Spirit is not present—by "heart" let us understand the deepest part of our being, our center, the place from which we make our most free choices.

The desire for good arising within us is the basic criterion for recognizing the transformation of our inner experience by the Holy Spirit. The theological reasoning supporting this truth is simple: we can make no movement toward good, toward God or others in love, by our own initiative; since the desire to love and serve God and others is definitely a movement toward good, it cannot come from our initiative; therefore it must come from God. The accompanying diagram is helpful to keep in mind during the remainder of this book. It sums up the basic criteria for recognizing the Spirit within our inner experiences.

The next diagram is more helpful than the self-in-God model of the person because it emphasizes the interaction of the three dimensions of our being. The Spirit in the diagram is at the center of the self. The Spirit represents our human spirit as well as the place where the Holy Spirit touches our human spirit. When our human spirit comes under the influence of the Holy Spirit, then our inner experiences of mind and body are transformed. The Spirit can transform our thinking and willing as well as our feeling and our imagining. Frequently every aspect of our inner experience is transformed by the Spirit. There are times, however, when our desires are transformed, though other dimensions of our inner experiences are not. Our criterion for infallibly recognizing the presence

## CRITERIA FOR RECOGNIZING THE SPIRIT

| *The Human Being* | *Direction of Heart* | *Source* |
|---|---|---|
| Body<br>Mind<br>Spirit | Toward desire to love and serve God and others<br>(Normally accompanied by peace) | Holy Spirit |
|  | Away from desire to love and serve God and others<br>(Normally accompanied by anxiety) | Not Holy Spirit |

of the Spirit within our inner experience centers on desires. Leaving the other aspects of our inner experiences aside, we are asserting that when our hearts are moving toward the desire to love and serve God and others, we are under the influence of the Spirit. This is true whether we actively make a conscious desire to love and serve or whether we are unreflectively and habitually moving with that desire. To get a fuller grasp of this rather simple criterion, it is helpful to spell out some of its implications.

It should be noted that although the movement toward love and service is normally accompanied by peace, the most reliable criterion for recognizing the Spirit is not situated either in inner peace or in the feeling of sensible consolation. First of all it is important to insist that the Spirit is present in our inner experiences even when our desire to love and serve is not accompanied by good feelings or sensible consolation. The Spirit may transform our desire but not our feelings. However when we experience a sensible consolation or good feeling accompanying our desire to love and serve God and others, then we can recognize the Spirit as transforming this dimension of our inner experience also. We know that our feelings can fluctuate from hour to hour and day to day. It cannot be stressed enough that the absence of sensible consolation in our feelings does not indicate the absence of the Spirit. When we desire to love and serve God even though we are feeling poorly, we are responding to the movement of the Spirit at our deepest level.

Nor is the experience of inner peace the best criterion for recognizing the Spirit's presence. The experience of peace is not exactly the same as the experience of sensible consolation; it is less connected to sensible feelings and more connected to a conviction that all is right between ourself and God and others. When this peace is present, we can say that the Spirit has not only transformed our desires but also other dimensions of our minds. Though inner peace *normally* accompanies the movement of the Spirit, it is not of itself an adequate criterion. There are times in our lives when situations overwhelm us and we are incapable of experiencing peace even though we are open to God and praying for peace, comfort and strength. When St. Paul speaks of the fruits of the Spirit as being love, joy and peace, he is making a very general statement. In short, inner peace of itself is not the infallible criterion for recognizing the presence of the Spirit.

There are also times in our life when God seems distant and our hearts seem empty of God's presence. Not only don't we have the confirmation of God's presence through sensible consolation and inner peace, but we even feel abandoned by God. During these times we yearn for God and for the return of sensible consolation and peace. And we continue to desire to love and serve God and others. At these times it is comforting to remind ourselves that as long as the desire for loving and serving God is present, we are under the influence of the Holy Spirit. Since by our own effort we cannot move ourselves toward the desire, we can conclude that the presence of the desire indicates the presence of the Spirit.

Finally we can recognize the presence of the Holy Spirit in our desire even in the midst of overwhelming boredom with our service to God, constant temptations, and almost complete inability to perform any spiritual activity with attention much less with devotion. In this state not only do we experience God as distant, but we experience ourself at all levels of our being as moving away from God. Often this state is referred to as "spiritual desolation." This experience can last for days, weeks, months or even years. It is important to be convinced of the fact that as long as the desire is present, God is present. For the desire flows from the deepest level of our being, a level deeper than the experience of the temptation, boredom and frustration with our spiritual life. We hang onto the desire to love and serve God with naked faith, with no support from the other dimensions of our being. Often this state is a prelude to a deeper union with God because it helps us purify our motivation. We learn whether we are loving and serving God for the peace and consolation this brings us or for God's own sake—whether we are seeking primarily the consolation of God or the God of consolation. As we surrender our attachment to peace and consolation, our hearts are purified and God emerges more clearly as the center of our lives.

It should be pointed out that our criterion for recognizing the Spirit joins together the movement of love for God with the movement of love for others. The reason for doing this is simple: all love is from God. Therefore the Holy Spirit can be recognized equally in love for others as in love for God. Jesus affirms this truth in his teaching of the two great commandments: the second, the love of neighbor, he tells us is like the first, the love of God. And it should also be acknowledged that love of self is equally from the Spirit. True self-love is different from selfishness. Selfishness ends in the self; true self-love is integrated with a desire to love and serve God and others. And Jesus commands us to love our neighbor as ourself. Jesus understood that if we loved ourselves because of our dignity as God's children, this love would naturally affect our attitudes toward all other people who are also God's children. Since true self-love is based on a desire to better serve God and others, it should be understood as being implicit in the criterion presented in the diagram.

A final comment on the diagram should be made. I have limited my discussion on the source of the desire to love and serve to the presence or absence of the Holy Spirit. The discussion has bypassed the treatment of good and evil spirits, angels and devils. It seems better not to get into a theological debate on the very important discussion over the effect of good and evil spirits on our motivation. Many people in presenting an outline for finding the source of motivation for good desires and actions would include good spirits and good angels. I have kept my diagram as inclusive as possible. The Holy Spirit as the source of good desires and actions can be understood to include good angels or good spirits, if one desires. It is always presumed, however, that these spirits and angels are operating as agents of God. Likewise our term ''not the Holy Spirit'' can be understood to include Satan, evil spirits, bad angels and devils as the source of bad desires and actions, if one prefers. The diagram implies that motivation away from God and others can arise simply from our own self-indulgence and need not be attributed to Satan and evil spirits. The diagram insists only that this inner movement is definitely not from God. What is crucial for Christian spirituality is that we recognize this bad desire. Whether we interpret this as coming from evil spirits, bad angels or Satan or simply the self outside the influence of the Holy Spirit is secondary in importance.

## The Holy Spirit in Daily Action

Using the criteria we have discussed, most of us will be surprised at the all-pervasive presence of the Holy Spirit in our daily life. Many of us have confined God's presence to certain activities clearly orientated toward God such as prayer, Mass and retreats. To get a better sense of the presence of the Spirit in our daily life, it is helpful to go through the regular activities of our day and see which ones are performed with a desire to love and serve God and which are not. There are two reasons for doing this: first, we want to recognize the presence of the Spirit in our daily life so that we can praise God for the Spirit's work in us; and second, we want to become aware of those activities where the Spirit is habitually absent in order to turn these activities over to the Lord and have them transformed. We have been called by Jesus to love and serve God and others with our whole heart and soul and mind and body. We can fulfill this command only by performing our daily actions in tune with the Spirit. We must now ask ourselves which of our daily activities normally fall under the influence of the Spirit and which do not.

Everyone's list will be different. I am presenting my regular daily activities for reflection only for the sake of giving an example. I am aware of how very different a daily schedule would be for a homemaker or a business person. I have chosen to list the activities I usually perform during a day when school is in session, and I am listing only the main actions of a typical school day. Having listed these activities, I will reflect on the presence and absence of the Spirit in them. *Early morning activities:* getting out of bed, showering, shaving, dressing, recording in journal, making morning prayer, breakfast. *Morning activities:* opening mail, doing office work, correcting papers, preparing class, teaching class, consciousness examen, attending or celebrating Mass, lunch. *Afternoon activities:* teaching class, office hours, academic and spiritual counseling, committee meetings, exercise, dinner. *Evening activities:* office work, correcting papers, counseling, attending university parties and functions, recreation with friends or students, evening prayer.

As I reflect on these activities, it is clear to me that some are done more habitually under the influence of the Spirit than others. My early morning activities are usually done with great peace and with the desire to love and serve God. However I occasionally wake up in a bad mood. The mood can arise from a dream, worry over the coming day's activities, frustration from the previous day. It is important that I become aware of the bad mood and deal with it by jotting in my journal, and perhaps also by using it as a starting point for personal prayer. I always try to leave my room with the desire to love and serve God uppermost in my mind. As I reflect on my later morning activities, I am immediately aware of activities in which the Spirit is not habitually present. The troublesome areas in my later morning schedule are usually opening the mail, doing office work and correcting papers. I find myself rushing to get these done, frequently with very little desire to love and serve others, and often becoming impatient and frustrated. Since I am both a faculty member and a chairperson of a department, I have a good deal of paperwork to do each day that is not directly orientated toward teaching, my own professional growth or serving others. On the other hand, I can usually recognize the Spirit's presence in my morning in the preparation and teaching of classes as well as making a consciousness examen, celebrating Mass and having lunch. I regularly do these with openness to love and serve God and others.

As I reflect on my afternoon activities, I see the Spirit present in my openness toward others in teaching, counseling and spiritual direction, as well as in the informal contacts I have with students and colleagues during my office hours. The trouble spot in my afternoon is committee meetings. I am on many committees and often get frustrated with the time the meetings take from my schedule as well as with the very slow movement of many of them. I intellectually know that the discussion is necessary to get consensus from the group, but nonetheless I become impatient and frustrated at the time spent before making decisions. Also troublesome is my daily exercise period. I often find myself resisting the exercise that I need and not approaching it with enthusiasm. Reflection on my evening activities indicates that I generally perform them with a true desire to love and serve God and others. This is true for the academic and spiritual counseling that I do as well as for attending student functions and recreating with friends. My lack of openness to the Spirit is noticeable during those evenings when I have much office work to finish or many papers to correct. I tend to resent all activities that are not directly aimed at serving other people.

In reviewing our daily schedule for the presence of the Spirit, it is necessary to pay special attention to the people we encounter. We attempt to become aware of relationships where we are habitually motivated by a loving desire to serve as well as those where this motivation seems to be absent. The list of significant relationships in our life always includes the following: immediate family, relatives, close friends, employers, fellow employees. Many of us also have significant relationships flowing from our neighborhood community as well as from our religious or civic communities; these should also be reviewed periodically.

In addition to becoming aware of the presence or absence of the Spirit in daily activities, it is helpful to become sensitive to those situations in our life that regularly can reverse our mood and move us away from the desire to love and serve God and others. Each of us knows that we can rise, begin a day with wonderful openness and then have unforeseen events occur which reverse the direction of our heart. These circumstances are limitless. It is helpful to know the ones which regularly occur so we do not allow them to reverse our attitude of heart: forewarned is forearmed. Some of the more typical ones in my day are the following: late night or early morning calls while I'm still in bed; continual interruptions during office work and class preparation; criticism of class by a student; discouragement over lack of response from class; irritation with idiosyncracies of selected faculty peers; criticism of my work by my superiors. Each of these situations happens with some regularity and I must be alert lest I allow these situations to reverse the direction of my heart.

## Two Prerequisites

By reviewing our daily schedule and our relationships we can get a general sense of the presence or absence of the Spirit in our life. Responding fully to the Spirit, however, has two key prerequisites: we must develop a lifestyle that fosters living in tune with the Spirit and we must not be afraid to face our evil inclinations. First, we must develop rhythms in our life that enable us to live in tune with the Spirit.[2] This condition is most difficult to fulfill, yet it is an absolute prerequisite for living the spiritual life in any depth. It may demand a rearrangement of our daily schedule. Most of us are very busy people; our time from morning to night is filled with obligations which may leave us very little time for other activities. The spirituality we are discussing demands not simply that we fulfill our responsibilities externally but that we discharge them in a way that reflects the presence of the Spirit in their performance. Our goal is to move through our day energetically, peacefully and lovingly in order that we may keep Christ's command to love and serve with our *whole* heart, soul, mind, and body. Three areas must be considered.

What adjustments should we make in our lifestyle in order to respond energetically to the Spirit and serve God with our "whole body"? Basically we must respect all the principles for keeping in good physical health. These include adequate sleep and rest, good nutrition and some regular physical exercise. We can serve the Lord with our "whole body" only if our body is in its best possible shape. With inadequate sleep and rest, poor nourishment and little exercise, we find ourselves becoming sluggish. This sluggishness may inhibit our responding to the Spirit energetically with our "whole body."

Should adjustments be made in order to live with more inner peace and so better serve God with our "whole mind"? We must respect all the principles fostering good mental health. A psychologically healthy person is one in touch with inner experiences and able to make free choices flowing from these experiences. The Spirit can influence and guide us only to the extent we are in touch with our inner self. Often, however, we are preoccupied with accomplishing our many duties and worried over our success. We live in a fear and anxiety that blocks our living in tune with the Spirit. Keeping in tune with the Spirit will then demand building sufficient time into our schedule to process our anxieties so that they do not dominate our consciousness. At times it may also demand seeking professional counseling for anxieties we cannot handle. Respecting the principles of psychological health enables us to serve the Lord with our "whole mind" as well as with our "whole body."

Finally, this prerequisite has implications on the spiritual level also. We must build time into our daily lives to be explicitly with the Lord and allow the presence of the Spirit to well up in our consciousness. This demands a regular rhythm of solitude, personal prayer, Mass and reflection on our actions. By setting time aside to be with the Lord we allow the Spirit to deepen our union with God and gradually transform every dimension of our inner experience. Only when our bodies and minds are under the influence of the Spirit can we fully respond to Jesus' command to love and serve God and others with our ''whole heart, soul, mind, and body.'' Living with this quality of heart presumes daily periods for reflecting on our motivation. During these periods we stop and orientate ourselves. If we find that we have not been serving the Lord wholeheartedly during the previous period, we adjust our orientation. Many of us have gotten in the habit of beginning each day with a Morning Offering. We know, however, that making the Morning Offering does not insure that we live our day for the Lord. Building periods of reflection into our day facilitates living this offering. Of course when we become aware during our day that we are not responding to the Spirit, we will automatically adjust our orientation. However if our service is flowing peacefully and energetically toward others, the presumption is that the Spirit is transforming it. We continue to serve the Lord without any self-conscious reflection on our motivation.

The second prerequisite for living in tune with the Spirit is acknowledging our evil inclinations. We all experience inner movements toward evil as well as toward good. Indeed the more we reflect on our inner motivation, the more it seems to be tainted with selfish desires; it may even seem that our evil inclinations have grown with our increased reflection on them. Most of us have a hard time admitting we have so many evil inclinations, preferring to think of ourselves as good people who have grown beyond the human foibles and selfishness we see all around us. Consequently we tend to strain from our awareness all our baser inclinations. But we must embrace the truth that we are human and that God permits humans to be tempted. From Adam and Eve it has ever been so. Each of us can expect to experience temptations arising from all the capital sins: anger, hatred, jealousy, envy, lust, sloth, gluttony. Experiencing temptations does not mean that we are evil; it simply means that we are human. Paul was tempted; Jesus also.

And it is important not to be afraid of these temptations. God permits us to experience temptations only because of the great good that can come from them. God remains present throughout the temptation, and with God's help no temptation need ever dominate our choice. In fact as we reject temptation, we affirm our desire to serve God and not ourselves; we imitate Christ in his explicit rejection of Satan's temptations; and we grow in union and love of God. God permits these temptations because they are such golden opportunities to deepen our commitment, but only if we acknowledge them can we use them to reaffirm this commitment. Paul understood the temptations in his life as being unique opportunities to experience the power of Christ. The following passage is the classic expression of the value of temptations in the Christian life:

> In view of the extraordinary nature of these revelations, to stop me from getting too proud I was given a thorn in the flesh, an angel of Satan to beat me and stop me from getting too proud! About this thing, I have pleaded with the Lord three times for it to leave me, but he has said, "My grace is enough for you: my power is at its best in weakness." So I shall be very happy to make my weaknesses my special boast so that the power of Christ may stay over me, and that is why I am quite content with my weaknesses, and with insults, hardships, persecutions, and the agonies I go through for Christ's sake. For it is when I am weak that I am strong (2 Cor 12:7–10).

## Growth in the Spirit

The principles for recognizing the Spirit apply at every stage of the spiritual path. Perhaps, however, the principles we are discussing are most applicable for those of us whose union with God is characterized by the experiences of the illuminative way. In the illuminative way the focus of our spirituality is no longer primarily on our external actions but on the internal quality of our heart, our purity of heart. Temptations occur, our heart fluctuates and, indeed, may move toward the temptation, but these temptations do not regularly get translated into external actions. Unfortunately many of us measure our sinfulness only by the conformity of our external actions to the example of Christ. Since our actions are not sinful, we believe we have no sin in us. I frequently hear the expression: "I don't go to confession because I have nothing to confess." When we make these statements we are usually referring to the fact that the external actions of our life are in conformity with Christ's example; however we are not adequately acknowledging the fact that there is a deeper level of sinfulness, one that relates to the quality of our heart underlying these actions. On this level there are none of us who can say we have no sin—other than our Lord and the Blessed Mother. Indeed as we become more and more aware of our quality of heart, we see elements of selfishness and sinfulness we never dreamed existed. And so as we travel along the Christian spiritual path, we are ever asking God to continue our conversion on a deeper level of heart. We are asking for the grace of a complete imitation of Christ that includes the transformation of our hearts as well as our actions and culminates in a total zeal for the service of God's kingdom uninhibited by our personal selfishness. Most of us are very far from this ideal. In this chapter we have examined some obstacles blocking the Spirit in our life. It is now necessary to review these obstacles in more detail and to outline practical means for recognizing and responding to them in our daily life.

## REFLECTION QUESTIONS

1. What attitudes do you notice in yourself and others that show the influence of the Western model in your understanding of Christian spirituality? Why do you feel that this model is so pervasive in your understanding of spirituality?

2. What criteria do you use to recognize the Holy Spirit in your inner experiences? What does this chapter add to your understanding of the role of the Spirit within your experiences?

3. Give examples from recent experiences in which you can recognize the Spirit at work in your desire to love and serve God and others even when this was not accompanied with sensible consolation and inner peace.

4. List the major activities of your day. Using the criteria of the desire to love and serve God and others, which are usually done under the influence of the Holy Spirit? Which are not?

5. List typical occurrences or interruptions in your day that are able to reverse the quality of your heart, that is, move you away from the desire to love and serve God and others.

6. List the various relationships in your life, personal as well as professional. Reflecting on the quality of your heart underlying these re-

lationships, which habitually manifest the presence of the Spirit and which do not?

7. Does your lifestyle foster living in tune with the Spirit? What patterns might be added or dropped on the physical, psychological or spiritual level to enhance your response to the Spirit?

# III OBSTACLES TO THE SPIRIT

We have focused our attention in the last two chapters on awakening to the presence of the Spirit and learning to recognize this presence in our inner experiences. It is now necessary to shift the focus slightly and to examine in more detail those inner experiences of our daily life that do not reflect the Spirit, in other words, those experiences where our heart is moving away from the desire to love and serve God and others. I have found personally that the primary obstacles to the Spirit in my life are my bad moods. Becoming aware of the causes of these moods is the most efficient way for me to get an understanding of these habitual obstacles. In this chapter we will discuss causes of our bad moods and then reflect on concrete ways of responding to them. Finally we will present a method for systematically reflecting on the presence and absence of the Spirit during our day.

## Acknowledging Bad Moods

A short cut for recognizing the absence of the Holy Spirit in our inner experience is becoming conscious of our bad moods and, in particular, the situations which cause these moods. We have seen that inner experiences are very complex, consisting of imagination, memory, feelings, thinking and willing. When we talk about a mood, we are simply putting an emphasis on the feeling dimension of these experiences. This feeling, of course, will be accompanied by the other aspects of inner experiences. We all experience an almost infinite variety of feelings from joy to sadness, from hope to despair. However we are concerned now with only one aspect of our feelings, namely, whether or not they are under the influence of the Spirit. And so we will be discussing good moods and bad moods. By a good mood we mean any feeling state that is under the influence of the Spirit because it supports our desire to love and serve God and others. By a bad mood we mean exactly the opposite: any feeling state that does not come under the influence of the Holy Spirit because it tends to move us away from the desire to love and serve God and others. Normally we can assume that a good mood would be accompanied by a feeling of peace and a bad mood by a feeling of anxiety. It is important to remember that our use of the terms "good mood" and "bad mood" refers to the presence or absence of the Holy Spirit and not merely to feeling good or feeling bad.

Why is it so important to deal with moods? We have insisted in the last chapter that moods are not accurate indicators of the presence or absence of the Holy Spirit. We have placed the reliable indicator of the Spirit's presence or absence in the will, or, more exactly, in the desire to love and serve God and others, and we have insisted that this need not be accompanied by a feeling. Nonetheless, in my experience it is helpful to center on our moods because they seem to influence our thoughts and actions more than any other dimension of our inner experiences. In other words if we are experiencing a good mood, that is, a feeling moving us to love and serve God and others, our thoughts and actions tend to be loving and peaceful. Contrariwise, if we are experiencing a bad mood, that is, a feeling moving us away from love and service, our thoughts and actions tend to be selfish and anxious. The key to controlling our behavior lies in becoming aware of our inner moods.

The question now becomes: What causes our bad moods? We must admit that we often find ourselves in these bad moods without ever consciously being aware of how they have occurred. Our challenge is to become more aware of the people and situations that cause these moods so that we do not unreflectively allow them to influence our thoughts and actions. For there is a very close link between causes, moods, thoughts and actions. To the extent that we become aware of the causes of our moods, we will be able to handle them and not allow them to influence our thoughts and actions. This truth is simple and obvious. Putting it into practice is very difficult, for bad moods can flow from an almost infinite variety of causes arising both from outside ourselves and from within our own personalities. After some reflection we can become aware of many of the sources. However no amount of reflection will uncover all of them because a lot of these sources are very deep in our psyche and are not available to us by ordinary reflection. Nevertheless it is helpful to become more aware of causes of our bad moods insofar as we are able.

We have said that bad moods are caused by sources outside of ourselves as well as deep within our personalities. It is really not very difficult to get in touch with the sources of our bad moods that are triggered by situations arising outside ourself. In Chapter 2 we tried to sensitize ourselves to the presence of the Spirit within our ordinary daily activities. We are now looking at these activities as the possible cause of bad moods. A quick review of the major activities of each day from the last chapter will pinpoint the causes of bad moods that are present in our daily schedule as well as in our daily encounters with certain people. However we must acknowledge that there are also patterns of events occurring outside our daily schedule that trigger bad moods. Without too much reflection we can look at the events of a typical week or month to discover which situations triggered bad moods. These situations flow from the various aspects of our life: sports, politics, religion, school, employment, family. In addition these moods may be triggered by such common occurrences as the weather, a toothache, a poor night's sleep, or disappointments as well as by serious misfortunes such as accidents, illness, and failures. Our goal is to become aware as far as we can of these causes so that we do not let them dominate our moods and affect our thoughts and actions. By reflecting on bad moods occurring regularly during our ordinary days as well as by reflecting on those moods which occurred during recent weeks or months, we can get a good grasp of the situations arising outside of ourselves that cause our major obstacles to the Holy Spirit.

It is rather easy to get an understanding of bad moods as they are triggered by situations outside of ourself. It is much more difficult to get an understanding of the sources of these moods as they arise from within ourselves. Each of us has a unique personality that is formed by inherited biological and psychological traits and conditioned by our family and cultural environment. This personality is the source of our strengths as well as our weaknesses. All of us emerge from childhood scarred in some way by our upbringing; we perceive the world through our weakness. Often we fail to respond objectively to situations, distorting events and perceiving them according to our own inner compulsions. I believe that the origin of most bad moods is within ourself, though they are often occasioned by events outside ourself. None of us ever fully understands our inner self, but the better we do come to understand it the more we are able to free ourselves from being controlled by our irrational anxieties.

Each of us has dominant characteristics that tend to distort our perceptions of life. I am aware that I personally have among my many destructive patterns an inferiority complex. I have described in Chapter 1 how this hurts my relationship with God. It also hurts my relationship with myself and others. I tend to judge myself inferior as a person because of bodily characteristics such as physique and appearance and personality traits such as intelligence and popularity. I find myself competing with others in order to feel superior to them and consequently better about myself. Yet I also need the approval of others for everything I do. Paradoxically this inferiority complex compels me to ''beat'' others while simultaneously expecting them to like me! I also find myself driven to be successful in my work; I am threatened irrationally by the slightest failure. As I gain more and more insight into my inferiority complex, I see how it pervades my perceptions of myself, others and God, causing many bad moods.

We all have certain dominant psychological tendencies that are major sources of our bad moods. I used to believe that everyone had the same set of weaknesses I had. Then I ran into a person who began describing an exactly opposite pattern. His constellation of weaknesses I summarize as a ''superiority complex.'' The patterns that flowed from it were the opposite of my own: arrogance and impatience, fear of dependency, fear of acknowledging personal weakness, lack of compassion for others' weakness. Initially I envied him for the strength and self-assurance his ''superiority'' gave him. As I got distance on the person, however, I saw how this constellation also cut him off from the type of relationship of closeness with people that mine seemed to foster—at least my need to be liked prompts me to extend myself to others. I decided that if we all had to have psychological problems, I would keep mine rather than exchange them for his.

We have seen that bad moods are caused both by situations outside of ourselves and by our own psychological compulsions. An important question now arises: Does God cause these bad moods? The answer to the question is no. Everything we have seen about the Spirit at work in our life shows us that when God does work in our hearts, God works always to lead us toward love and service. Bad moods which cause temptations away from love and service are not from God; they are exactly the opposite of how God works. We can, however, say that God does allow or permit us to experience these moods and the temptations that arise from them. Indeed if God did not permit these, they would not happen. But just as quickly as we assert that God permits these moods and the temptations that flow from them, we must add that God's grace is always with us to help us through them. We are never left to face our bad moods and temptations alone. In every situation the grace of God is stronger than the temptation toward selfishness. We don't know why God made us so susceptible to bad moods and temptations; but we do know that since God is love, God must have judged this to be better for us. Perhaps St. Paul comes the closest to giving us a reason for the temptations we experience. Paul tells us that the Lord spoke to him when he pleaded to have his temptations removed, and the Lord said, "My grace is enough for you: my power is at best in weakness" (2 Cor 12:9). Each temptation gives us the opportunity to freely choose God over self-indulgence and to experience God's strength in our weakness.

> So I shall be very happy to make my weaknesses my special boast so that the power of Christ may stay over me, and that is why I am quite content with my weaknesses, and with insults, hardships, persecution, and the agonies I go through for Christ's sake. For it is when I am weak that I am strong (2 Cor 12:9–10).

We must keep this truth of God's presence in temptation in mind especially when we experience little peace or joy in our service. It is a common experience that during certain periods God seems distant or absent. We continually examine our life to see whether or not we are blocking this presence by our conscious, sinful patterns. Examine as we may, we are not aware of situations that are clear obstacles to God's grace, yet sensible consolation and peace are not present. These periods are frequently called "dark nights" by spiritual writers. They can produce feelings of frustration that tempt us to throw up our hands and give up in our service of God. We feel that since we are getting nothing from our service in terms of consolation and peace, we need not be so conscientious. This can be one of the greatest trials in the spiritual life. However the very fact that we desire to experience again the Lord's closeness assures us that God is present. We do know God never stops loving us: "Does a woman forget her baby at the breast, or fail to cherish the son of her womb? Yet even if these forget, I will never forget you'' (Is 49:15).

It is very important to distinguish an experience of guilt or remorse for sin from the experience of a bad mood. Each of us has areas in our life where we are not struggling as we should to live in the Spirit. In these areas we have more or less decided to go along with our sinfulness. In order to transform our hearts and lead us back to the desire to love and serve, the Spirit now works in our conscience to arouse in us a sense of guilt and remorse. This remorse is very different than a bad mood: bad moods prompt us away from the desire to love and serve God and others; guilt and remorse, however, prompt us toward love and service by making us uncomfortable with our sinfulness.

Finally it should be noted that we are not always able to know the causes of our bad moods. Much of our motivation is buried in a way that may never be available to us by ordinary reflection; yet it can continue to exercise an influence on our feelings. This is especially true of events of early childhood. But it is important to recognize the bad mood even if we are not sure of the cause. When we acknowledge and name the mood we take away its power to dominate our feelings. The paradox of spiritual growth is that as we grow in union with the Lord, we seem to experience our sinfulness more acutely. This of course does not mean that sinfulness was not present in the earlier stages of our growth; it simply means that at these earlier stages, especially before our awakening, we were not sensitive enough to recognize these tendencies. However the ultimate reward for openness to our sinful tendencies is always greater intimacy with the Lord. Each time we acknowledge our brokenness and bring it to God for healing, we have a new opportunity to experience God's love and power.

### Responding to Bad Moods

The spiritual life is simple when we are enjoying a good mood. We flow spontaneously toward God and others with the desire to love and serve. However we know that we do not live consistently in good moods. The crux of the spiritual life is recognizing bad moods as soon as they occur. At these moments we must examine ourself, making sure that the mood does not influence our thoughts and actions. The following five pieces of advice have helped me deal with my bad moods effectively.

First, name the bad mood. This means that as soon as we are aware that something is wrong—usually indicated by restlessness or anxiety—we must stop and ask whether we are experiencing a bad mood. This presumes, of course, that we are living a rhythm of life that enables us to be sensitive to our inner experience so that we can become aware when something is wrong. The sooner we name the mood as bad the better it will be for ourself; for then we refuse to allow the temptation arising from the mood to influence our thoughts and actions. If we do not name the mood as bad immediately, the temptations arising from it will then flow into our subsequent behavior. Since bad moods are not under the influence of the Spirit, we are unwilling to allow them to flow into activities. I will illustrate the five pieces of advice by using a very typical example in my own life. The example is receiving a criticism about a class from a student. The criticism frequently triggers a bad mood in myself. I exaggerate the criticism and become depressed—my inferiority complex makes me ultra-sensitive to any criticism. To protect myself I am tempted to undervalue the student's criticism and respond defensively. This temptation may flow out into action, and I may deal with the student impatiently, suggesting that the student is not doing enough homework to understand the class adequately or that the student is not paying full attention in class. However if I acknowledge that the criticism has triggered a bad mood, I will not allow the temptation flowing from the mood to flow out into my actions. I will then attempt to understand what the student is saying and see if I cannot use this to improve my class. I will also attempt to be grateful to the student and help the student in any way that I can.

Second, replace the bad mood with a good desire. Having named our mood as bad, we attempt to substitute a good desire so that our behavior flows not from our bad mood but from our good desire. We recall that the most reliable sign of the presence of the Spirit in our inner experience is the desire to love and serve God and others. When we replace our bad mood with a good desire, we are doing all in our power to align our deepest center with the action of the Holy Spirit. Indeed levels of sinfulness remain buried in us, but we can only deal with what we are aware of. Often our mood does not change immediately and it is necessary to live with the bad mood. At these times we can be comforted by the knowledge that our deepest identity flows not from the mood but from our desire. Having replaced the bad mood with the good desire and allowed this desire to influence our behavior, we have done all we can. For instance, in my treatment of the student who has just criticized me, I must allow my desire to love and serve that student to affect my behavior and not my bad mood. Frequently, however, after I have named the mood as bad, I find it disappearing; my good mood is restored and with it my desire to love and serve the student. I am then spontaneously able to treat criticism with care and concern for the student's welfare.

Third, work against the bad mood as much as possible. If the mood arises in the midst of a busy day, we simply replace the bad mood with a good desire and go on with our duties. We postpone dealing with the mood fully until we have more leisure. At that time we try to get at the cause of the mood. It is helpful to know the cause in order to apply the right remedies for removing the mood. For instance, if the cause flows primarily from some physical dimension of our nature, then we will have to deal with it at that level. We all know that physical tiredness and exhaustion can cause bad moods. Dealing with this source of a bad mood may simply mean taking a nap in the course of the day or going to bed earlier the following evening. But if the mood flows from some psychological cause, we will deal with it in a different manner. Very frequently our own personality needs distort our objective evaluation of the situation. For instance, when I am criticized by a student, my inferiority complex comes into play. I tend to overreact to the criticism and to permit myself to become unduly discouraged. Dealing with a mood flowing from this source demands that I reflect to see whether my reaction to the cause is objective. I must put the criticism of the student in context, seeing whether it adequately reflects the opinions of a majority of the students or whether it may flow from the student's individual frustration. It should be added that physical tiredness often renders me more vulnerable to criticism. Dealing with bad moods often involves both the psychological and the physical levels of our being.

Whatever the cause of my mood, it is important to involve the spiritual level also. Working against the mood always means bringing it, if only for a moment, to the Lord and asking for healing. Recalling the Lord's presence in the midst of the mood gives strength to handle the temptations arising from the mood. Though the bad mood may remain present, the power of Christ's grace in us is stronger than the temptation; consequently our actions need never be determined by the mood. At this point we can identify with St. Paul boasting in his weakness: ''So I shall be very happy to make my weaknesses my special boast so that the power of Christ may stay over me'' (2 Cor 12:9). In short, working against the mood implies dealing with it on all three levels of our existence: physical, psychological and spiritual. Eventually the process of dealing with bad moods becomes habitual and spontaneous: we become familiar with their causes, instantaneously recognizing the moods and just as instantaneously applying the proper remedy. We become more like Jesus, rejecting the temptations in our life the way he rejected those in his: ''Be off, Satan! For Scripture says: 'You must worship the Lord your God, and serve him alone' '' (Mt 4:10).

Fourth, do not allow the bad mood to influence behavior. The goal of the spiritual life is to respond to the Spirit working in our heart; we know that bad moods do not come from the Holy Spirit. If we allow them to influence our behavior, we are not responding to the Spirit but yielding to temptation. In general this means that our behavior should be the same after the bad mood arises as before. For instance when I am criticized by a student, I am tempted to be resentful of the student and to allow my actions to reflect this resentment. To assess whether the mood has affected my behavior, I can ask myself whether I am treating the student in the same way after the criticism as before. If I am not, then I have violated the norm I have just presented. Indeed if my behavior does change, it ought to change in a way to show more love for that student. That way I can be sure that my reaction is not flowing in a subtle way from my resentment of the student.

Fifth, recall that God's strength is always sufficient for dealing with our bad moods. We must remember that a bad mood is not a sign that God is absent from us; it simply means that God's presence has not transformed the feeling dimension of our inner experience. Often when we are under the influence of a bad mood, especially if the mood has persisted for some days, we may conclude that God has abandoned us and that we do not have the strength to deal with the mood. It is crucial to recall that God never abandons anyone; God's only desire, for even the worst sinner, is that we repent and return. This is a very important dimension of the story of the prodigal son. God does not turn away from habitual sinners; all the more God does not turn away from conscientious Christians experiencing fleeting bad moods. We are comforted with the same knowledge that comforted St. Paul: nothing can come between us and the love of Christ.

For I am certain of this: neither death nor life, no angel, no prince, nothing that exists, nothing still to come, not any power, or height or depth, nor any created thing, can ever come between us and the love of God made visible in Christ Jesus our Lord (Rom 8:38–39).

## Practical Format for Daily Examination

Christians have always recognized the necessity of some regular form of daily examination of actions. For Catholics this is formalized in the examination of conscience preceding confession. During this review we conscientiously examine the previous period to see how well we have been living the Gospel. In a less formal way we say evening prayers, including in them a review of actions of the day. Some of us have grown up with the habit of making a Morning Offering before we begin our day. Many events can happen to reverse the good intentions with which we began our day. The review we are suggesting aims to see whether we have lived the offering we made in the morning. Traditionally we have called the reflection on our life "examination of conscience." The term implies that we examine our day in light of the particular actions which were good or bad. The focus was, however, on the actions themselves. The review we are suggesting is more appropriately called "consciousness examen."[1] The focus of this review is not primarily on the actions but on our consciousness or attitude of heart with which we perform them. This examination is concerned with recognizing a consciousness that reflects the presence of the Spirit in our day as well as with recognizing the consciousness that does not. In other words, it is aimed at getting in touch with our good moods so that we may thank God for the presence of the Spirit as well as with our bad moods so that we will not be dominated by them. Throughout all of our reflections we have been insisting on the close connection between mood and action with the belief that from a good mood good thoughts and actions will flow and from a bad mood bad thoughts and actions. Looking at our moods rather than our actions is a more effective way to recognize God's presence or absence in our day.

The consciousness examen that is most helpful for myself contains five moments: prayer to the Holy Spirit for enlightenment, thanksgiving, examination of moods, contrition, and resolution. The order of these five moments may vary. If our day has been basically peaceful and lived in response to the movement of the Spirit, the order flows as presented above. After the opening prayer we focus on thanksgiving to God for the presence of the Spirit in our day. Having done that we move to examination of bad moods, contrition for failure to serve and firm resolution for the following period. However if the day has not been peaceful but rather marked by the presence of bad moods and anxiety, our examination assumes another order. After the opening prayer for guidance, we focus on the moment of examination of bad moods. The turmoil of our heart demands that we deal first with what has been bothering us. After the examination we move to contrition and resolution. Finally having dealt with the problems and anxieties of the day, we may be able to move to thanksgiving. I believe it is important to acknowledge the quality of heart with which we begin our examen and allow this to determine the order of our examen rather than to force it into a preconceived format. The goal of our review is to become aware of how the Spirit has been working in our inner experiences. This goal can be achieved without a rigid format, a format that may stifle the action of the Spirit. What I am presenting takes between ten and fifteen minutes. For the purposes of this discussion I am presuming that the review is being made at noontime.

We open our consciousness examen with a prayer to the Holy Spirit for enlightenment. The purpose of the entire reflection is to allow the Holy Spirit to emerge in our consciousness and reveal where we have been responding to God's Spirit and where we have not. The review cannot be done successfully without the Spirit. However evoking the Spirit in our consciousness is not always an easy task. To do this effectively requires that we withdraw from external activity as much as possible, find a place of solitude where we can listen to our heart, and then allow the Spirit to emerge and influence our reflection. As we stop in the middle of our busy day we find our bodies relaxing and our minds slowing down: we are experiencing God and the whole quality of our inner experience is being affected. We are now in the presence of the Lord who affirms us with this presence during our reflection as well as guides us into a knowledge that will facilitate our living in response to the Spirit during the rest of our day. If we come to our review immediately from a bustle of activity, it will take longer to become situated in God's presence. This is all the more true if we come to our review from activity that has been rushed, frustrating, anxious. Slowing down and evoking

God's Spirit is absolutely indispensable for an effective consciousness examen. The noon examen is a Spirit-guided review of our morning; it is not simply self-centered introspection. If the Spirit is present, the review will always be peaceful and refreshing.

The second moment of the examen is the moment of thanksgiving. We find ourselves moving rather naturally into this moment if the morning was filled with the signs of the Spirit's presence: peace, love, joy, patience. We desire to thank God for the presence that has brought this peace amid our activity. In the mood of thankfulness we allow the blessings of the morning to emerge. This can be done in two ways: we may allow the Spirit spontaneously to evoke these blessings or we may choose to run through our morning schedule systematically. As more and more events occur to us, we understand how active God has been in our life. We see God not only sustaining our mood of inner peace but also touching us through the people and situations of our day. On many days, especially those days when there have been few anxieties, we may choose to spend most of our examen simply resting gratefully in the presence of God. There is no need to rush through this moment of thanksgiving to reach the subsequent moments of examination, contrition and resolution because we know that we have responded well to God's presence in our morning. Our re-creation during these examens comes from becoming ever more aware of how we have been blessed by God.

The third moment of the review is the moment of the examination of bad moods. There are two parts to this examination, the general examen and the particular examen. In the general examen we look at the entire morning to get in touch with bad moods and actions flowing from them. In the particular examen we review a previously chosen trouble spot of our life to see how well we have handled it in the preceding morning.

The general examen is our attempt to get in touch with our bad moods and their causes and reflect on how they have been influencing us. There are two ways of making a general examen. If the morning has been rather peaceful with no particular bad mood or behavior standing out, we may systematically review the major periods of the morning to see if we might not have overlooked some bad moods and actions. Often, however, it is not necessary to make this systematic review. The cause of our bad mood is immediately obvious. We then review it to see how it has affected the morning. After this we may or may not want to reflect systematically on the actions of the morning to see if there have been other bad moods.

The length of this general examination will vary from day to day. If we have spent the morning peacefully, we may find it sufficient to reflect only briefly on the events of the morning. However if the morning has been marked by great anxiety, we may find it necessary to make the major part of our consciousness examen on the causes of the anxiety. It may take a while to become fully aware of what has been bothering us. Peace can be restored only after we have acknowledged our bad moods and actions and humbly gone to the Lord for healing. Therefore the goal of spending an extended time in this part of the examen is not only to give the Spirit time to reveal our sinfulness but also to heal our sinful hearts. It is my experience that getting in touch with the causes of our bad moods is not that difficult. Most of us are aware of the situations and relationships in our life that precipitate them. As we quiet down and review our morning, these situations and relationships become painfully obvious. We also examine these moods seeing whether they were precipitated by some new situation we have not adequately handled and whether they were caused primarily by our own compulsions.

The second part of the examination is the particular examen. In the particular examen we review the morning in light of a particular problem that has been disturbing us and causing the most bad moods in recent days. Often one relationship or situation is the primary obstacle to the Spirit; the purpose of this examen is to set up a plan for dealing with the obstacle when it occurs. The most effective way of dealing with it is clearly to specify the situation that is causing the bad mood and just as clearly to formulate constructive thinking and behavior to substitute for the destructive thinking and behavior. The particular examen is aimed at substituting thoughts and actions that flow from the Holy Spirit for those that do not. The key to the success of a particular examen is concreteness. For instance, if I am being criticized continually by a group of students for a prayer course I am teaching, I name the course and name the individual students who are doing the criticizing. I then choose a behavior to substitute for my destructive thinking. The behaviors I choose are usually scriptural ejaculations rather than any external actions—

though sometimes this is also necessary. I record my particular examen in my journal the following way:

Situation:    Criticism of prayer course especially by John and Mary.

Behavior:    The Lord is my shepherd, I shall not want.

During the particular examen I review the morning to see how I handled the situation. Did I recall my ejaculation in situations either in or outside class when I was criticized for my conduct of the class? Generally if I recall my particular examen during an actual encounter with these students, I will not let my bad mood influence my actions. I will substitute the good desire to help these students for the temptation to an uncharitable reaction flowing from the bad mood. The particular examen should be kept for as long as the situation continues to be the dominant obstacle blocking the Spirit in our daily life.

The fourth moment of the consciousness examen is the moment of contrition. This moment emerges naturally after the general and particular examen. As we become aware of our bad moods and actions we naturally want to present ourselves to the Lord for forgiveness and healing. The length and intensity of this moment of contrition will vary day to day. If we have spent the morning radically out of tune with the Spirit, we will want to rest humbly before the Lord, asking for a conversion of heart and healing. The moment of contrition is to our bad days what the moment of thanksgiving is to our good days—an opportunity to express our relationship to the Lord and to be affirmed by the Lord's presence. On our bad days we are affirmed as forgiven sinners; on our good days we are affirmed as blessed children. On our good days the moment of contrition may be very brief since we have not experienced our sinfulness acutely. On these days it is more natural simply to rest in thanksgiving to God for all our blessings.

The fifth moment of the consciousness examen is the moment of resolution. The purpose of this moment is to look ahead to the afternoon period. We do this for two reasons: first, we want to visualize concretely the coming period and renew our desire to serve God and others during it; second, we want to see if there are any situations that may arise that are usually troublesome. We visualize the situations so that when they do occur we will not allow them to affect our quality of heart: forewarned is forearmed. This moment of examen is especially important on our bad days. The moments of examination, contrition and resolution are very closely connected: we become aware of our sin, express our sorrow to God and resolve not to repeat it. Hopefully we emerge from the consciousness examen confident that our grace is stronger than our sin and so we need not be dominated by our sinful inclinations.

On days that we experience a great deal of anxiety flowing from bad moods, we move directly from the opening prayer to the Holy Spirit to the moments of examination, contrition and resolution. On these days we do not include the moment of thanksgiving immediately after the opening prayer to the Spirit because our hearts are dominated by our awareness of sinfulness and we experience an urgency to deal with this sinfulness. Having done this, however, it is good to include the moment of thanksgiving at the end of the examen. We become poignantly aware that through all our infidelity, the Lord is faithful. We want to thank the Lord for this fidelity, even in spite of our sinfulness. We may also recall blessings from the morning that we have overlooked because of the dominance of the bad mood. On these days, then, the moment of thanksgiving may emerge naturally as the final moment of the consciousness examen.

## Come Aside and Rest Awhile

The time spent during the consciousness examen is a time of peace because it is a time spent with the Lord. I often experience my noon examen as an island of tranquility in the midst of a busy and hectic day. Intensifying and reestablishing contact with the Spirit is always refreshing. The consciousness examen will be distasteful only if done in an overly introspective and self-centered way. If we find ourselves resisting the consciousness examen, we might ask ourselves whether we are doing it in a way that is, indeed, allowing the Spirit to emerge and transform our consciousness. It may be necessary for us to adjust the circumstances in which we make our examen to make sure that, first, we are giving ourselves enough time to allow the Spirit to emerge and affect our consciousness and, second, that we are making the examen in a place that is quiet and facilitates listening to our inner movements. If we make the consciousness examen properly, we can expect to experience the fruits of the Spirit: charity, joy, peace, patience. Who of us could not use more of these gifts in our day?

The question now arises: How often should we make a consciousness examen? The answer to the question will vary according to our personal needs and daily schedules. I myself find the following rhythms most helpful. I examine myself at the beginning of each day before breakfast in order to become conscious of my mood. I am in a habit of keeping a spiritual journal, and I record my moods and my particular examen in this journal. If I am dominated by a bad mood, I prepare myself to deal with that mood through the particular examen. I find that the process of jotting in my journal followed usually by personal prayer confirms my heart in the Spirit, and I can usually leave my room with the desire to love and serve God and others. I do not, however, make a formal consciousness examen at this time.

The most important time for me to make a consciousness examen is at noon. My examen usually takes fifteen minutes. However this varies according to the time I have available and according to my own personal needs. It is very important for me to make this examen. If I have been dominated by a bad mood during the morning, I can adjust myself so that the mood does not affect the afternoon. I frequently discover during the examen that I have been rushing and worrying throughout my morning and really not performing my jobs with a full desire to love and serve God and others. It is only at noon when I consciously stop to reflect on my morning that I become aware of this quality of my heart. As I reorientate myself, peace emerges.

Finally, I make a brief examination in the evening as part of my night prayer. It is usually a simple resting in the presence of the Lord, being grateful for the blessings of the day. In the evening I am usually too tired to go through the regular process of examining my day in terms of the presence and absence of the Spirit. I find that I can do that more effectively the following morning when I am jotting in my journal. However I do find it beneficial to stop in the evening before going to bed to recall God's blessings. This puts my mind at peace and facilitates a more restful night of sleep.

Jesus tells us that the goal of our life is to love and serve God and others with our whole heart, soul, mind and body. But there are times of great stress and anxiety in our lives that make this very difficult. During these times we may need longer and more frequent periods for the consciousness examen. Ideally examens should be made as often as is necessary to align our hearts with the movement of the Spirit. We know that the Spirit is the treasure of which Jesus speaks in his parable. This treasure is the kingdom of God; it is buried in the field of our heart. Jesus tells us that we must arrange all our life around the seeking of this treasure.

> The kingdom of heaven is like treasure hidden in a field which someone has found; he hides it again, goes off happy, sells everything he owns, and buys the field (Mt 13:44).

After our awakening to the Spirit within ourselves, we Christians are the ones who have found this treasure. We happily arrange our lives to seek it, for without it our lives are empty and meaningless. We build rhythms for making the consciousness examen into our daily schedule not because of some obligation imposed upon us by an external authority but because we desire to live in tune with this treasure. We come aside and we rest with Jesus during the examen only to walk more closely with him after the examen.

## REFLECTION QUESTIONS

1. Describe how you usually handle bad moods. Is this similar to or different from the approach presented in the chapter?

2. List the people and situations connected with your personal life that occasion bad moods in you. Does your handling of these people and situations reflect the five pieces of advice given in this chapter for responding to bad moods? Explain.

3. List the people and situations connected with your job that occasion bad moods in you. Does your handling of these people and situations reflect the five pieces of advice given for responding to bad moods? Explain.

4. Describe the personality traits you observe in yourself that most frequently cause bad moods to arise. Do you handle the bad moods aris-

ing from these psychological causes according to the five steps given in the chapter? Explain.

5. List the bad moods which arose in your heart today. Did you respond to them according to the five pieces of advice given? Explain.

6. What is the dominant obstacle causing bad moods in your life now and blocking your response to the Spirit? Arrange a particular examen to deal with it.

7. Describe your regular rhythm for reflection on your life. Compare and contrast this with the patterns given in this chapter for (1) the format of the consciousness examen and (2) the frequency of this examen.

# IV SEEKING GOD'S WILL

The goal of Christian spirituality is to live in tune with the Holy Spirit so that the Spirit can direct our life. In the first three chapters we have discussed a general method for recognizing and responding to the Spirit in our daily activities. But allowing our lives to be directed by the Spirit has another dimension; we must allow the Spirit to guide us in the important decisions in our life. We are now asking whether by reflection on our inner experiences we can be guided by the Spirit to discover God's will in these decisions. The answer is "yes." The purpose of this chapter is to present a method for finding God's will by reflecting on inner experiences. However before discussing the method, it is important to clarify the meaning of God's will as we are using it in this chapter. Having done this we will proceed to list the conditions that must be present in order to use the method effectively.

## Meaning of God's Will

Does God have a will for us? A very brief reflection on the New Testament answers that question with a strong "yes." Jesus tells us that he seeks always to do his Father's will, and Jesus teaches us to pray that this will be done on earth as it is in heaven: "Thy kingdom come, thy will be done on earth as it is in heaven." What then is God's will for us? Traditionally our understanding of God's will has been broken into two categories: God's universal will binding on all and God's particular will for each individual. There is general agreement that God does have a universal will binding on every human being. God wants us, first of all, to live in harmony with our human nature. God's will can be found through the correct use of our reasoning by reflecting on what is and what is not in accord with our human nature. In addition to this we know that

God also wills that we live according to the example and the teachings of Jesus. Indeed the very reason for God's sending Jesus on earth is to reveal more fully to all humankind how God wants us to live. Finally we know that God also wills that we obey lawful authorities in our life both within and outside the Christian community. In short we can know God's universal will through right reason, divine revelation and properly constituted authority.

Our purpose, however, is not to discuss God's universal will. In this chapter we are asking whether in addition to this God has a particular will for individuals.[1] Catholics most frequently put the question in terms of vocations. Does God give some people vocations to the priestly and religious life, some to the married life and some to the single life? Is this vocation, then, God's will? I believe there is a consensus in the Christian community that God does have a will for individuals that includes a call to a particular ministry in the Church. Christians have found support for this belief in the New Testament. Jesus calls some of his followers to leave all things and follow him in a special way; we think of the calling of the apostles as well as the calling of the rich young man. We Christians have traditionally understood these aspects of the Gospels to imply that God does call some people to serve the kingdom in different ways than he calls others. However Christian tradition has always emphasized that all vocations are holy because all come from God. The holiest calling for the individual is the one the Lord has given the individual.

I believe there is a second consensus in the Christian community regarding God's will for individuals. God's call is God's preferred way for the individual to serve the kingdom, but God does not punish individuals for not responding to it. For instance Jesus extends the invitation to the rich young man to follow him, and the rich young man refuses the invitation. Jesus does not then proceed to banish the man from the kingdom. Since the vocation God gives each of us is God's preferred way that we serve the kingdom, we also believe that it is our path to greatest effectiveness in the kingdom and to greatest personal fulfillment and happiness. We definitely do not believe that refusing to respond to the call means exclusion from God's love and a life of unhappiness and frustration.

At this point in the discussion of God's particular will for individuals a new question arises: Does this will include only the general vocation of the individual or does it also include particular choices within that state of life? There is no general consensus within the Christian community as to the extent of God's will for particular choices. My personal position is that God has a will for us regarding choices that bear *significantly* upon service to God's kingdom. My reason for this belief is simple: God wills the fullest coming of the kingdom into this world and can achieve this coming only through the work of individuals under the guidance of the Spirit. I believe that the Spirit is sent by God to guide individuals to make the most effective choices for the kingdom. I believe that these choices include major decisions such as changes of ministry as well as minor ones such as decisions for service within one's current ministry. However my belief of the extent of God's will for individual choices is surely not a general consensus. Every reader at this point in our discussion must make a personal decision regarding his or her belief about the extent of God's will. Does God direct us only in major choices such as decisions to change ministries or jobs, or does God also direct us in other types of choices such as making decisions within our particular ministry and job? My position is that God does direct us to make choices in our ministry and jobs that bear significantly on our service to God's kingdom.

To illustrate the conditions and methods for finding God's will, I will use two examples from my own life. The first is not controversial: it is my own experience of deciding to become a Jesuit priest during my senior year of high school. In addition to illustrating the method through this example I will illustrate it through a more controversial example. I believe that God guides me in making choices which bear *significantly* upon my service to the kingdom. A choice I must regularly make is which opportunities to serve within my current ministry I will accept. I will discuss a recent decision I made whether or not to accept an invitation to give a four-evening lecture series during Lent. I consider a decision such as this to be a significant one because it implies setting aside large amounts of time both to prepare and to present the series. It is typical of many decisions I must make. Each time an invitation such as this is extended, I must ask whether God is calling me to take time out of my already busy schedule to serve the kingdom in this new way.

I have entitled this chapter "Seeking God's Will." *Seeking* is an unpretentious word; I have used it deliberately, preferring it over several alternatives: *finding, discovering, knowing. Seeking* implies that, as far as possible, we are building into our decision a process that leaves maximum room for the Spirit to guide us; but it also implies that due to our own limitations, we may seek but not find this will. We are limited in our ability to discover God's will by many factors; these factors will become clearer throughout the discussions of the conditions and methods for seeking God's will. They usually cluster around our lack of openness to God's will and our inability to get in touch with the inner experiences that may be leading us to this will. I must humbly admit that in many personal choices I make I cannot always say I have found God's will; however I am always comforted by the fact that as far as I was able I did seek to discover it.

## Conditions for Seeking God's Will

In order to use validly the method for finding God's will, there are certain conditions that must be present. In fact it could be argued that if these conditions are present, there is no need to use the method because the will of God will emerge naturally. There are five conditions; they overlap one another. First, we must believe that God does indeed have a will for us in the decision. Second, we must believe that God will reveal this will through a conscientious reflection on our inner experiences. Third, we must desire to know that will and not simply have our own inclinations confirmed. Fourth, we must intend to carry it out when it is made known. And fifth, the decision must be in conformity with God's universal will as known to us through other channels. This last condition is an important point for all our reflections. The method for finding God's will we are discussing is not a method for getting around God's universal will as known by moral reasoning, Scripture and legitimate authority. We are seeking in this method to discover an indication of God's will when we have a decision to make between two or more alternatives all of which are good in themselves and in conformity to God's universal will.

To begin any search for God's will we must believe first of all that God does indeed have a will for us in this particular choice. This presumes that we have previously formulated a position regarding the extent of God's will in our lives. For instance before I could decide to seek God's will for becoming a Jesuit, I must believe that God does, indeed, have a will for me in this regard. Likewise for the four-evening Lenten series. Since it is my belief that God does have a will for me on decisions bearing significantly on service to God's kingdom, I must then see the choice on the Lenten series as a significant choice.

Second, I must believe that God will reveal his will to me through conscientious reflection on my inner experiences. Throughout this book we have been discussing the role of the Spirit within our inner experiences. We are now extending this activity of the Spirit to leading us through these same experiences to God's will. We are asserting that by reflecting upon our thinking, willing and feeling we can receive an indication of this will. It is important to note that the method we are presenting does not look outside our own experiences for some external sign from God; the sign from God will be contained in a special quality of our own inner experience and not in some external event. We are not denying that God's will can be revealed through dramatic private revelations. Indeed this has happened with saints and privileged individuals. However this is not God's normal way of acting. Should God act in this way we have no need to use this method.

The third condition is that I must truly want to know God's will rather than simply have my own initial inclinations confirmed. This is the most difficult condition to fulfill. It presumes that I want to be free from all influences on my decision that do not proceed from the direction of the Spirit. All of us are influenced in our decisions by many forces. To find God's will successfully we must be aware of these forces and see how they are influencing us, but we must not allow these forces to determine our conclusion without reflecting on them. We must be especially aware of three influences on our decision that may impede our freedom. The first is the influence of our culture and immediate environment. We are all products of the groups to which we belong and our thinking is in large measure influenced by these groups. We must be aware in seeking God's will that we simply do not thoughtlessly make judgments that are conditioned by the habitual preferences of the group, whether this group be our family, friends, religious or civic community. It is helpful to be aware of the preference of the group, but we must scrutinize this preference by holding it against the inner experiences necessary for finding God's will. Second, we are all influenced in our decisions by our inner dividedness, what we have called the tension between the Spirit and self-indulgence. Often we find that our initial inclination is to do what seems to be most gratifying to ourselves without considering whether this is from the Holy Spirit. And the third force that can influence us is rationalization. We can use our reasoning to justify the decision that we are initially inclined toward; this tendency toward rationalization often flows from our self-indulgence. We can even bolster this initial inclination by claiming that it has the support of prudence. We are, indeed, capable of doing this with the best intentions.

To fulfill our third condition it helps greatly to be aware of all three of these forces. If we are aware of them, we can process them. However if we are not aware of these forces, we may unreflectively accept them as indicating God's will. If we are listening to our deepest self, the will of God can emerge even amid these conflicting forces. But we must learn to listen to our "heart" and not our "head." When we are in contact with our heart, the deepest dimension of our being, we are in contact with the Spirit and the Spirit can transform our thinking, willing and feeling. At the level of our heart we may find ourselves reaching a different conclusion than we reached on our thinking level; our head is more likely to be influenced by forces from our environment and our sinfulness and rationalization. The Spirit is the strongest force within us, stronger than sinfulness. When we reach our heart, the Spirit has the power to point us beyond our superficial desires and reveal God's will.

My decision to become a Jesuit priest involved transcending all three of the forces I have indicated. I was aware of two conflicting desires. First I had the desire to go to college, become a lawyer, raise a good Christian family and continue to enjoy the type of life I had known. This was my dominant desire. But I also experienced another desire: to join the Jesuits. I had a very happy experience in my Jesuit high school. I was attracted to many aspects of the Jesuit life, and I could see myself joining the Jesuits and helping high school students in much the same way they had helped me. There were, however, aspects of this life that were not attractive to me, such as poverty and the lack of a family. My problem during the second half of my senior year was to decide which of these two desires was from God. At this time in my life I did not make a formalized reflection. As I look back now, however, I can see how much of my thinking was conditioned by the forces that were playing upon me. My cultural conditioning surely pointed me toward getting a college education, becoming a successful professional and enjoying Christian family life. This was what almost one hundred percent of my classmates would be doing. I believe this conditioning was reinforced by my own selfishness and desire for "the good life." I can even remember fantasizing about taking my large Christian family with me to Hawaii on vacation. I was quite bright and had decided that I would have a very flourishing career and become wealthy. Finally I can see that I also used a process of rationalization to keep me from being open to God's will. I reflected on the fact that I could do much good for God and the church by raising a good Christian family and contributing to the Church, especially with the generosity that my abundant financial resources would make possible. Indeed when I reflected seriously on my future life in January of my senior year, I decided that God was calling me to go the path of college, law school and Christian family. I even sent the deposit to the university assuring me a place in the freshman class.

In March of my senior year my decision changed. In the midst of all my thinking I was still drawn toward trying Jesuit life. There was something deep in me that said it was more right for me even while I was in the process of talking myself out of it. I simply could not work up a great deal of enthusiasm for the decision I had made in January, nor did I experience peace when I reflected on this decision. In March of my senior year, then, I decided that it was more right for me to apply to the Jesuit novitiate than it was to begin college. As I reflect now on the decision I made in January, I can see that I did not find God's will then because I was not open to it. I wanted to have my own initial inclination confirmed. I was subsequently able in March of my senior year to come to a decision to apply to the Jesuits only because I listened to the voice deepest within me. I believe that at that point I had been freed by the Spirit to transcend the forces of my environment, selfishness and rationalization and was moving with the Holy Spirit toward God's will. I was finally listening to my heart and not my head.

Likewise in making the decision to accept the four-week Lenten series I had to be freed from similar forces. My initial inclination whenever I am asked to do extra presentations is usually negative; I am already very busy and cannot easily add other extra obligations and still be faithful to my prior commitments. However I have learned that this initial inclination is not always the indication of God's will; it is often the result of my rationalization which leads me to conclude that I am already doing all that I can with my energies for the kingdom. If I listen to my head and not my heart, I will usually respond negatively to requests for my services. I recall having these negative inclinations when I was asked to do this Lenten series. I have learned that I must give myself several days before responding to such requests in order to allow myself to listen to my heart. During these days I pray to be freed from any selfishness that might obstruct being open to God's will. This waiting period may or may not confirm my initial inclination. In the case of the four-week Lenten series it went against my initial negative inclination. In this decision also my heart contravened what my head was saying. I gave the Lenten series believing that this was indeed God's will for me.

The fourth condition that must be present is closely related to the third: I must intend to carry out God's will when it becomes known to me. An indication that we really desire to know God's will is our determination to implement it when it becomes known. We cannot, for instance, be led to God's will if we have decided that we are willing to do anything God asks of us except, for example, to enter the full-time ministry. When some such reservation is present God will not even be able to draw us to that alternative. By refusing to budge from a deeply held precondition, we are putting obstacles to the Spirit that may be insurmountable. I believe that this was what I did during January of my senior year. I recall praying intensely to God to know God's will; I also recall vigorously putting the idea of joining the Jesuits out of my mind whenever it occurred and turning my attention to going to college and getting married. I was not open to God's will at that point, nor did I have any intent to carry it out should it be made known to me. I wanted to know God's will only if it confirmed my inclination to go to the university.

A fifth and final condition must be present to use our method validly: the particular decision we are making must be in conformity with God's universal will as it is known to us through ordinary channels. We are concerned with alternatives for serving God, all of which are good but one of which is better because it is in conformity with God's will. The method we are proposing is not a method to make choices that are at odds with God's will as it is known to us through ethical reasoning, Scripture and properly constituted religious and civil authority. This is not to deny that a conscientious Christian may make choices that are at odds with God's universal will known through these channels. It should be acknowledged that often God is moving people to use civil disobedience and conscientious objection to some laws. Jesus himself did this. However I am simply asserting that the method we are presenting does not have this type of decision as a focus. The two examples we have been discussing are obviously compatible with God's universal will as known through other channels. Neither is an attempt to get around the conclusion of moral reasoning, revelation or properly constituted authority.

## Method for Making a Decision

If the conditions are present, we are safe in proceeding to use the method. However we often experience that the conditions are not fully present, but it is still necessary to make a decision. Usually the condition that is most wanting is the desire to know and implement God's will; often we enter the decision-making process primarily to confirm our own initial inclination. As long as we know we are not totally free in seeking God's will, it is safe to proceed to use the method; using the method is the most helpful way I know to come to greater freedom to want God's will even over our own will. I entered the process of decision-making regarding my vocation and the Lenten series with an initial inclination to have my own will confirmed. It was through the process itself that I gradually came to desire to know and do God's will rather than have my initial inclinations confirmed.

There are five steps in the method.[2] The first step is the formulation of the proposition to be reflected upon. The next three steps are very closely related; they are reflection on the proposition using our minds, our wills, our feelings. The fifth and final step is confirming the decision made through the method. I will illustrate this method primarily by using the example of my decision to give a four-week Lenten series. I used the method about to be described in making this decision. I will also illustrate the method by referring to my decision to apply to the Jesuits. However it should be emphasized that this decision was made thirty years ago and was not made using the method to be presented here.

The first step of the method is the formulation of the proposition to be reflected upon. There are two directives for doing this most effectively. First the proposition must be stated as concretely as possible. Since we intend to carry our decision into action, it is important that all the specific details be included in the proposition; otherwise we will not know just exactly what God is calling us to do. The initial formulation of my proposition read as follows: "I will give a four-week Lenten series on Personal Prayer at St. Mary's parish on Monday nights." This statement contained all the pertinent facts for my decision: what I would do, when I would do it, where I would do it. Further concrete details were implied in this statement; I had exact dates specified for me as well as the hours on which the series was to begin and end.

The second directive for formulating the proposition effectively is that it be stated in a way that God initially seems to be drawing us. This directive respects the fact that the Holy Spirit is already working within our experience and may indeed have already transformed our inner experience to give us an indication of God's will—the very fact that we desire to use a method to seek God's will in this decision implies that it is an important factor in our life. I find it most helpful to state the proposition positively. In this decision I was asking God to indicate to me whether or not I was being called to give a series on prayer. I had leeway for choosing the topic for the series and I was initially drawn to presenting a series on personal prayer. Hence I formulated the proposition that way. As my reflection evolved, I changed the topic from Personal Prayer to Finding God in Daily Life. It was, however, important to begin my reflection with the way I was initially leaning. Only in the course of being open to the Spirit working in my inner experience did the new topic emerge as being more in conformity with God's will. In our statement of the proposition we are not concerned that all the details be solidified; they should simply reflect how we feel the Lord is drawing us at the present time.

I should note that I had not fulfilled all the conditions for using the method appropriately; I entered the reflection with prejudice against doing the series. However I am aware that this is a rather habitual prejudice for me and arises any time I am asked to add a significant amount of work to my already busy schedule. I did state the proposition affirmatively because I have learned from experience that my prejudices are often not in tune with God's will. I also stated it affirmatively because in recent years God has led me to give an annual Lenten series as a way of serving more generously during the Lenten period. I have substituted this extra service to the Lord during Lent for the prescribed fasting we traditionally did. On the basis of my past experience, I judged that the Lord might be calling me to give another series even though my initial inclination was not in that direction.

The decision I was being called to make was rather simple; I was choosing between two alternatives. Oftentimes a proposition is not ready to be stated because there may be several possible alternatives, and we are not aware of how we are most strongly drawn. I am continually counseling college students who are deciding what God is calling them to do with their life following graduation. The typical alternatives open to the ones who come to me involve the following: further studies in graduate or professional school, volunteer work for a year, applying for a job, religious or priestly vocation. The students who come to discuss these alternatives are usually concerned with choosing God's will for their life. If I can see this disposition in the student, I will ask them to go through the following process. First I ask them to list all the alternatives that they see as possible for themselves for the coming year. Then I ask them to make a list of pros and cons for each of the alternatives after they have reflected upon them for a period of time. Having completed this, I ask them to rank the alternatives in the order of preference as they currently experience them. Finally I tell them to use the alternative ranked first as the proposition for the formal reflection on seeking God's will by the method we are presenting here.

These preliminary steps are necessary whenever we experience more than one alternative open to ourself. I frequently use that same method to decide how to spend my summer months. The alternatives regularly open to me are the following: teaching at Creighton University, teaching at another institution, writing articles and preparing courses at Creighton University, writing articles and preparing courses at another institution, applying for post-graduate study. Reflecting on these alternatives in terms of their pros and cons and then ranking them in order of preference is a great help for me to formulate the final proposition to be decided on for the following summer. The process allows me to get in touch with the many motivations that are at work in me; some are flowing from the Spirit and some definitely not. I also use the method to decide which courses to teach in a given semester.

The second step of the method is using our minds to reflect on the proposition. This has two parts. First, we want to call up into our awareness all the reasons that incline us against the proposition and all the reasons that move us toward accepting the proposition. It is helpful to make two lists: first the con list with the negative reasons directly under it and second the pro list with the reasons supporting the proposition directly under it. It is important for me to list all the reasons that bear upon my thinking. Many of these reasons clearly do not flow from the influence the Holy Spirit: many of them flow from my own selfishness and from outside pressures. But by listing all the reasons I can get a better grasp of the forces that are influencing me. It is especially important for me to list all the reasons when I have begun my reflection without a complete desire to know and do God's will. If I can isolate those forces on me that are not flowing from this desire, I can better evaluate them and determine what influence they should have on my decision. This way they will not be able to exercise an influence on the final decision without my being aware of it.

The second part of the reflection is the formal evaluation of all the pros and cons to see which of them seem to be flowing from the influence of the Holy Spirit and which do not. The listing of the pros and cons and the evaluation of these should go on over a period of days or, if the decision is major, weeks or months. If we make the list hurriedly during one sitting, we are likely to be in contact only with what is dominating our consciousness at that time. However if we make the list over a period of days and weeks, we will have a better likelihood of being in contact with a fuller range of motives within ourself. Eventually the list of pros and cons stabilizes and we are able to recognize motivations coming from the Spirit and those which do not. The following lists were written in my journal as part of my reflection on the four-week Lenten series.

Proposition: I will give a four-week Lenten series on Personal Prayer on Monday nights at St. Mary's parish:

*Cons:*

already giving two workshops in Lent

crowded schedule

given prayer series three times before at St. Mary's

given four other series already this year

*bored with prayer series

need time in Lent for self and prayer

*Pros:*

good Lenten penance for myself

series in Lent worked out well in previous years

St. Mary's is a central location in city

Monday nights in Lent free for me

little preparation needed for prayer series

desire to provide adult education in town

need more time for preparing courses

I'm already overworked

is this a workaholic tendency

*give series on Finding God in Daily Life

*Finding God: better preparation for new book

*gave this series (Find-God) only once before

series requested by several already done series in previous years with success

chance to sell more copies of my book

chance to make money for community

take place of fasting during Lent

heighten my service to the kingdom during Lent

*After changing topic to Finding God in Daily Life I added these to the Pro column.

As I reflected on the above lists, I became aware that some of the reasons listed did not flow from the Holy Spirit. The most obvious of these were under the Pro column, namely, chance to sell copies of my book and chance to make money for the community. But as I reflected on the two columns, I became more sure that I was indeed being called to give a four-week Lenten series. I was comfortable with every detail of the proposition but one, the topic of the series. Even though the topic of personal prayer would require far less preparation and therefore far less time from my schedule, I was uncomfortable with it. I found that when I substituted the topic Finding God in Daily Life I was peaceful with the proposition. I changed the topic of the proposition and then transferred several reasons from the Con column to the Pro column. I noted I had more enthusiasm for giving this series than for giving the prayer series. But at this point I still had two desires in me: the first, to stay home, prepare class, rest and pray more as part of my observance of Lent; the second, to give this four-week Lenten series as a way to increase my service to God. Here it is important to note that God's will need not necessarily be identical with the conclusion of a prudent reflection process. In my case prudence may have dictated that I stay home and spend more time in prayer since I had already accepted other commitments for Lent. It was now necessary for me to watch which way my will was being drawn when I reflected on the pros and cons of giving this series.

The third step of the method is observing the direction of our will when we reflect on the reasons for and against the decision. It is clear how closely connected step three is with step two: as we gain illumination from the Spirit on the reasons for and against the proposition, we simultaneously find our will being moved by the Spirit in one or the other direction. This makes sense, for we know that our inner powers work together; we can expect the Spirit simultaneously to transform our thinking and our willing. If we are making our list of pros and cons over a period of days, we may find our will fluctuating one way and then the other as we add to our list. Eventually, however, we find our will resting more comfortably on one of the alternatives. In my decision on the Lenten series my will did not rest comfortably on doing the series until I had changed the proposition. However after I switched the topic, I found my will resting consistently on the desire to give the series. If we have begun our reflection without total openness to God's will, it is likely that our will may move back and forth. Identifying our selfish inclinations is the first step toward not allowing them to influence our decision. The days we are making the lists, then, can become a period of purification; we decide whether in fact we do want to know and implement the Lord's will more than having our own initial inclinations confirmed. Here I must quickly add that it is always possible that what we might have judged selfish is really flowing from a good self-love and the Spirit is indeed calling us to do something for ourselves.

It is important to note that the will is not drawn toward one alternative or the other simply on the basis of the length of the lists. If this were the case, the decision would merely be the result of a prudential judgment; we would decide to go along with the alternative that had the longest list of good reasons. This, however, is not what happens in the process. As we reflect on the list, certain elements of them become more important to us than others. As I reflected on my original list, two reasons stood out. The first was in the Pro column: giving a Lenten series is a wonderful way for me to intensify my service to God during Lent. This factor seemed more important to me than the fact that prudence might dictate I keep some more time for myself since I was already busy. The second element was on the Con list: over a period of days my will was drawn toward the topic of Finding God in Daily Life. Even though this topic would require much more time to prepare and might seem to be against a prudential judgment, my will continued to be held toward it. I believe my will was being held toward it because it was now aligned with God's will. The feeling of rightness was the result of my will resonating with the drawing of the Spirit within myself. Often there can be long lists of pros and cons but it will be only one or two entries on the list that are compelling in making the decision. And the decision may not seem to be in line with prudence or common sense. Serving God may involve the risk of losing our job, reputation and friends; it may involve a call to generosity that is beyond a normal conventional practice of Christianity.

A note on my decision to apply to the Jesuits. In January of my senior year, having prayed to know God's will, I decided that God was asking me to attend college and raise a good Christian family. However during the following two months I was aware that my will was not held toward that alternative. My will seemed to be drawn toward applying to the Jesuits. This occurred even though I was vigorously trying to put the Jesuits out of my mind. Only in March of my senior year did I end my resistance and decide to take the first steps in the application process for joining the Jesuits. From March until my entry into the Jesuits in August my will was held rather consistently toward this alternative. I believe that it was held this way because it was now aligned with God's will.

The fourth step in the method centers on our feelings: we ask the Lord to give us the feeling of sensible consolation on the alternative that is more for God's greater glory. The middle three steps of the method are closely connected: we ask the Spirit to enlighten our mind to know God's will; then we ask the Spirit to draw our will toward God's will; and finally we ask the Spirit to give us sensible consolation for the alternative that is in accord with God's will. The Holy Spirit is progressively transforming each of these aspects of our inner experience. The transformation of our feeling through the gift of sensible consolation is the final criterion for knowing God's will. At this point God not only directs our will toward a decision but also confirms this decision with sensible consolation.

An important clarification must be made on the use of feeling as a sign that God is pointing us toward a particular decision. Often we enter a decision not totally desiring to know God's will and our feelings are pointing us away from seeking God's will. Indeed this was the case in the two examples I have given. My initial inclination was away from doing the Lenten series and from applying to the Jesuits. The feelings we are now talking about are those which emerge as we progressively purify our motivation under the influence of the Holy Spirit. These feelings are the ones that accompany our desires when they are clearly pointed toward loving and serving God and others; they are far different from the feelings that accompany our desires aimed only at our own self-indulgence with no reference to loving and serving God and others. The process of using this method often involves a transformation of feeling. At the end of the method we find ourselves emerging with a certain enthusiasm for the very alternative to which we were closed at the beginning of the method. And just as the will fluctuates during the use of the method, so do the feelings, especially if we have begun the method without a clear desire to know and do God's will. In the course of both the decisions we have been discussing, my feelings were gradually transformed. For instance after I switched the topic for my Lenten series from Personal Prayer to Finding God in Daily Life, I began experiencing a certain amount of sensible consolation and enthusiasm for that decision. Likewise, after I had reversed my decision not to join the Jesuits and had decided to apply, I began experiencing consolation and enthusiasm for that alternative. Significantly from January to March of that year, I experienced no sensible consolation or enthusiasm for my decision to attend the university, become a lawyer and raise a good Christian family.

The presence of sensible consolation when I reflected on joining the Jesuits was absolutely crucial for giving me the strength to make this decision. In retrospect it seems as though the Lord "tricked" me through this means to get past my own selfishness. Beginning in January of my senior year I began experiencing consolation during prayer in a way I never experienced before in my life. Indeed this was the beginning of my awakening to the Holy Spirit. I recall going up to church, sitting in front of the Sacred Heart altar and being absolutely overwhelmed. This was the first time I had ever experienced this type of enjoyment from being with God. And this consolation was present whenever I reflected seriously on the possibility of entering the Jesuits. If I began to lose this desire, I would simply return to my parish church, sit in front of the Sacred Heart altar, and again that consolation would be given me. Throughout this period I knew instinctively that this was the right decision for me because of this consolation. I had not the slightest knowledge of a technical process for finding God's will by reflecting on my inner experience nor did I have the help of a counselor. I simply had a confirmation of sensible consolation. It is because of this particular experience that the method I am proposing makes so much sense to me.

It should be noted that the same sensible consolation was experienced, though in a far less degree, in my decision to do the Lenten series when I changed the topic to Finding God in Daily Life. Since my mind, will and feeling were now resting comfortably with the decision to do this Lenten series, I made the judgment that this was God's will for me. However this is not the final step in the process. The fifth step is to live with the tentative decision to see whether our mind, will and feeling will continue to be held toward this alternative over a period of days, weeks or months, depending upon how important the decision is.

## Confirming the Decision

The fifth and final step in the method is confirmation of the decision that has been made. Basically this means accepting the tentative decision as God's will and living with the decision over a period of time. We live with the decision for two reasons. First, we want to observe our inner experience of mind, will and feeling to see whether they continue to be drawn toward the decision. If the decision is truly from the Lord, usually our minds will find more reasons to support it, our wills will be held toward the decision and the feeling of consolation will accompany our thoughts on our decision. This drawing of mind, will and feeling occurs as frequently outside of prayer as during prayer. Often we are simply struck with the fact that what we have decided is right for ourselves. Since this conviction arises spontaneously in us with no preparation on our part, we know that we are being held toward the decision by the Holy Spirit and not by our own will.

Second, we want to live with the decision for a period of time in order to observe whether we have used the process adequately. We will want to check to make sure, first, that all the conditions for making a good decision were present and, second, that we conscientiously used all the steps of the method. There are many reasons why tentative decisions are not confirmed. Perhaps the main reason is that we entered the process seeking primarily to have our own inclination confirmed and not to know and do God's will. This is especially true if we made the decision with great enthusiasm because it was something that we deeply wanted; we presume that since we seem to want this so badly, God must also want it for us. It is also true if we make the decision too quickly. Oftentimes we don't get a clear indication of God's will, and we are worn down by the process of asking how God is leading us. When we finally make a decision, it comes as a relief from the effort of trying to decide between two alternatives. The relief is experienced as consolation from the Lord, whereas it really is simply a psychological result from ending a trying decision-making process. Further in the period after a tentative decision has been made, we may discover some new circumstance that influences our conclusion and undermines the decision. Also if a tentative decision has not been confirmed, it is possible that the formulation of the proposition did not include God's will as one of the alternatives. It is even possible that God does not have a will for us in this matter at this present time. And, finally, even though we consciously desire to seek God's will, it is very possible that we are being motivated on a subconscious level in a way that does not permit us to be open to God's direction; we think we are free, but we actually are not. It may be necessary for us to have some outside help to discover this lack of freedom and deal with it.

For these and many other reasons we may find our mind, will and feeling fluctuating away from the tentative decision. The presence of this fluctuation during the period of confirmation is an indication that we may not, in fact, have discovered God's will. However this does not mean that we were wrong to proceed in making this decision. Often we don't get the data we need until we have made a tentative decision and then found it was not confirmed. At this point in the process we have received important new data and can now redo our decision in light of this data. We can reformulate our proposition and put it through the same process and see whether or not the alternative formulation is eventually confirmed by God.

My experience of deciding to join the Jesuits illustrates many facets of these observations. In January of my senior year during a retreat I looked for God's will for my life after high school. I decided that God was calling me to go to college, become a lawyer and raise a good Christian family. I recall experiencing some relief at having finally come to a decision. This decision, however, was not confirmed by the Lord; the Lord did not hold my mind, will and feeling toward it. As I reflect on it now, I can see clearly that the necessary conditions for seeking God's will were not present: I wanted to know God's will only if it confirmed my initial inclination toward going to college and getting married. I noticed that during this time my will was constantly pulled away from this alternative and toward the alternative of applying to the Jesuits. In addition I felt no inner peace much less sensible consolation and enthusiasm when I thought about going to the university. In March of my senior year I finally gave up the struggle. I decided to apply to the Jesuit novitate. From this time to when I entered the novitiate in August, I had an entirely different experience. I consistently felt peace and sensible consolation whenever I reflected upon entering the novitiate. I intuitively judged that this peace was an indication that I was doing what was most right for myself.

However as I reflect back on that whole process, I am convinced that it was very important for me to make the wrong decision first. It was only because the decision I made in January was not confirmed with the feeling of peace and consolation that I changed it. Had I not made that decision in January, I would have lived with the two alternatives constantly present in my mind and not have made a formal decision for either one. Most likely I would have drifted into college. It was also important for me to make a tentative decision to give a Lenten series on the topic of Personal Prayer. It was only my unease with this aspect of the proposition that led me to revise it and change it to Finding God in Daily Life. At this point my mind, will and feeling were held toward the decision. But I could not have done this without the previous wrong decision.

Perhaps a note should be added on how we know that the experience of consolation accompanying a decision is indeed a sign that this is the Lord's will. This truth is not revealed as such in Scripture nor taught formally by the Church. It is, however, presented as a criterion in *The Spiritual Exercises of St. Ignatius*. Several prominent theologians have reflected on why this criterion might be valid.[3] These theologians ask why we should experience consolation when reflecting on a particular alternative for serving God. There is no natural reason we should experience this, especially if the alternative we choose is initially at odds with our personal preference and even seems to be at odds with a prudential judgment. Since we cannot explain this enthusiasm for the decision from natural reasons alone, they conclude that the peace and joy we experience emerge because our will is now resonating with God's will: God's Spirit has joined our spirit. This touching of our hearts by the Spirit is the sign God gives to us that we have indeed discovered

God's will. As might be expected this period of confirmation will vary in length of time. For major decisions it may be weeks or even months; for minor decisions it may be several days. My decision to give the Lenten series on Finding God in Daily Life was confirmed within a week's period of time. I believe my decision to apply to the Jesuits was confirmed over the entire period from March to August. Had it not been confirmed by the experience of sensible consolation, I believe I would have changed that decision.

Three cautions should be made regarding the experience of peace and joy during the confirmation. First, we can look for this experience only during the moments when we are in contact with our deepest self. Often during a period of confirmation we will not be in tune with our center and we may find that this experience then recedes. In order to be sure that God is indeed calling us to a decision, we must provide time during the confirmation period to be quiet before the Lord and allow the Lord to touch our heart with peace and consolation regarding the decision. I recall that I experienced many doubts in my own decision to enter the Jesuits between the period of March to August. But whenever I went to the church and sat in silence, my experience of peace was restored and with it the conviction that God was calling me. Since God speaks to us in the depths of our heart, we must listen to our hearts and not merely to our heads. Our heads are more influenced by the external pressures from our environment and our own personal dividedness.

The second caution is that we may be drawn away from a decision because of our fear of the decision. If the decision is major, we automatically tend to put up more and more obstacles to making it. Our heads then can provide doubts about the decision that may undermine our feeling of peace and consolation. To cope with this fear of making big decisions, we must break the decision into smaller parts. We then decide to take the "next right step" for ourself. This bit of advice was very important to me for making my decision to apply to the Jesuits. When I applied to the Jesuits, I had not decided that God had called me to be a Jesuit priest for the rest of my life. I had simply decided that it was more right for me to apply to the Jesuit novitiate than it was to go to the university. I applied to the novitiate to see whether or not I was being called to the Jesuit life; I felt that if I experienced the life I could then make a better decision. In the back of my mind I thought that I need only experience the life for a few weeks in order to make the decision: the novitiate started August 8 and the university September 18. I recall deliberately deciding not to request that the university return my deposit. I intended to leave the novitiate and enroll at the university if it did not work out. My experience of consolation accompanied my decision to try the novitiate for this period; I am not sure whether this experience would have accompanied a decision to be a Jesuit priest for the rest of my life. In all major decisions we simply attempt to make the "next right step" for our life. If we are moving toward the marriage vocation, we proceed through the steps of dating, going steady, becoming engaged and, finally, getting married. If Catholics are moving toward the religious and priestly vocation, they proceed through the steps of application, temporary vows, permanent vows and, for some, ordination. We reach the ultimate goal of our life's journey one step at a time; God can lead us to this goal step by step by confirming each decision along the way.

The third caution regarding sensible consolation is that we must make sure that it originates from the decision itself and not from some other factor. It often happens that we make bold and generous decisions for the Lord when we are full of consolation. The consolation, however, may proceed from some other factor than from the fact that our will is aligned with God's will. Frequently we have important religious experiences and in the afterglow of these experiences make generous commitments to our Lord and even decide to enter the religious or priestly life or full-time ministry. However as the consolation enjoyed from the retreat fades, we may find that our mind, will and feeling may no longer be held to the decision. This may mean that the consolation we experienced did not originate from the fact that our will was aligned with God's but originated from some other source, even though it remains valid spiritual consolation.

Some may ask: Why bother to seek the Lord's will if we so frequently have such difficulty finding it? If we are awakened to the Spirit, the answer is simple: we want our whole life to be led by God. If there is a possibility that God wants to lead us toward a particular practical decision, we want to give God's Spirit maximum room to operate. And even though we don't always find God's will, we experience peace in the knowledge that we have tried our best. And when we have found God's will and our decision is confirmed, we approach living out of the decision with an entirely new attitude. Since this is what God wants, we perform it with new assurance: God will strengthen us in doing it; there is nothing better or more perfect that we could do for God now in our life than simply carry out this decision. For instance I know that God has called me to live my life as a Jesuit. There is nothing more perfect that I can do for God than being a good Jesuit; and since God has called me to this vocation, God will give me all the strength that I need to live my vocation well. On the level of our less significant decisions, we have the same assurances. For instance there is nothing better that I could do for God on Mondays during Lent than give this particular Lenten series. Since God has called me to give this series, God will give me the wisdom and strength to perform it well. If I experience doubts about having made the right decision as I get closer to the series, I recall that I made the decision conscientiously and the decision was confirmed by consolation. I evaluate these doubts as not flowing from the Spirit but from myself outside the Spirit. I then put them aside and throw myself energetically into doing God's will.

### Directed by the Spirit

Seeking God's will for significant decisions may seem unduly complex. In my own life I am able to simplify and apply this method regularly by following two pieces of advice. I find myself giving this advice frequently to others—and to myself. First: ''Listen to your heart and not your head.'' I know my heart is the place where God speaks directly to me; my head is the place where I am most influenced by pressures outside myself and by my own internal dividedness. And second: ''Take the next right step for your life.'' I cannot be sure what the future holds for me; I can only decide to do what is the next right thing for me now. I trust that the big decisions in my life will fall into place as I conscientiously make my small decisions looking for God's will every step of the way. I have found much peace abiding by these two pieces of advice. I know there is much good I can do for God's kingdom in many different parts of the world. I frequently become anxious because I feel I am not doing enough. But I also know that the best service I can perform for God's kingdom is that to which God calls me. The dialogue between myself and God is simple. I often pray the prayer of Samuel in the Old Testament: ''Speak, Lord, your servant is listening.'' And I seem to hear the response God gave to the servant in the Old Testament: ''You are my servant whom I have chosen, my beloved with whom I am pleased.''

## REFLECTION QUESTIONS

1. Explain your position on God's will for individuals. Does God have a will for individuals in addition to his universal will binding on us all? If so, how far does this particular will extend? To vocations only? To major decisions within a vocation? To significant service for God within a vocation? Compare your position with the one presented in the chapter.

2. Recall a major decision in your life. Describe the method you used for making this decision. Explain how God's will entered your decision-making process.

3. If you explicitly sought God's will in this decision—or any other decision you recall—compare and contrast the method you used with the conditions and method presented here. What ideas from this chapter would you like to add to your decision-making processes?

4. Have you ever sought God's will without really being open to it? Explain. How did you discover you were not open?

5. What criteria do you use to judge that you have found God's will for a decision? Give examples. How do these criteria relate to the ones given in the text for the confirmation of the decision as being God's will?

6. Is God's will for individuals able to be equated with the conclusions of common sense and prudence? Explain your position. Compare and contrast it with the position presented in the chapter. Have you ever been called to do something that seemed at odds with prudence and common sense? Explain.

# V KEEPING A SPIRITUAL JOURNAL

I have been keeping a spiritual journal for fifteen years; it is the most important spiritual activity of my day.[1] I find that no matter how busy I am, I never omit jotting in my journal. There is no other single spiritual activity I perform that serves the function of orientating my life toward the Spirit in the same way that the journal does. For this reason I place the highest priority in my daily schedule in setting aside time for keeping this journal. Everything I have discussed in the first four chapters of this book finds its way into the journal. The journal is the place, first of all, where I reflect on my good and bad moods. It is also the place where I formally note a particular examen for the coming day. And it is the place where I record the pros and cons in my attempt to seek God's will for particular decisions. Since the journal has been so important for myself in accomplishing the goals of responding to the Spirit, it seems right to conclude this book by sharing my experiences with it. I will begin by describing the gradual evolution of my practice of recording the journal, then give my method for making my daily recordings, and finally present the content of these daily recordings. The chapter will conclude by explaining the use I make of these recordings for monthly days of recollections and for annual retreats.

## Use of Journal: Personal History

The practice of recording in my journal has evolved significantly over the past fifteen years. Since the journal had never been presented to me as an important part of my spiritual life, I want to describe how I personally discovered its value and how it assumed its role as my most important daily spiritual practice. During the first five years of my journal keeping, I slowly discovered that I had a great need for the help the journal can give; for the last ten years it has been my most important daily spiritual activity. But during the entire period the use of the journal always responded to a felt need in my life. The need has varied. At first it was to simply get my anxieties expressed on paper so I could clear my mind and get on with the work at hand. It gradually evolved into a need to integrate my life more fully with the Spirit so I could perform my daily activities with greater peace and love. I can testify that I never kept the journal because I felt I had to—the journal had never been presented to me as an important component of the spiritual life. I kept the journal because I wanted to; it enabled me to live my life in greater peace.

I began my journal in October 1971. The previous month I had made an Intensive Journal Workshop given by Dr. Ira Progoff.[2] Though I had made the workshop, I had not adopted immediately the technique given in the workshop for keeping a journal. I had a good experience during the workshop, but felt I was too busy to adopt the journal-keeping technique presented. The method I am presenting in this chapter is related to, but not identical with, the method presented by The Intensive Journal Workshop. It was the workshop itself that gave me the first experience of centering and recording the moods that evolved from the centering. I discovered during the workshop that as my bad moods evolved and as I recorded them on paper, I was able to deal more effectively with them. Dealing with them, then, enabled me to be more free and peaceful in performing the regular activities of my day.

During this time I was in the throes of writing a doctoral dissertation. I had secluded myself in an out-of-the-way seminary room to write for five hours a day. This writing turned out to be the most difficult and exhausting intellectual task of my life. Many mornings I would arrive in the room and find it impossible to start writing; my mind simply would not work. I would stare at the typewriter and manuscript, but no thoughts would come. I had an immense emotional investment in finishing this dissertation; I saw my whole future life as a college teacher of theology evaporating before me should I not finish. In retrospect, I can see now how this anxiety tended to paralyze me. It was in the midst of this paralysis that I decided to use the technique I had learned in the journal workshop for dealing with inner fears and anxieties. I got a notebook and began recording my feelings about my dissertation. Each morning when I arrived in the seminary room, I jotted down all the anxieties I was experiencing about the dissertation in general and especially about the particular part of the dissertation I intended to write that morning. After I had expressed these anxieties, I began planning in the journal the writing I hoped to do that morning. I discovered that after I had dealt with my very negative moods I was far more free to move toward positively planning my writing for the day. And it worked. I would soon put the journal aside and begin typing my dissertation. I kept this practice from October 1971, to July 1972. I successfully completed my dissertation and made my teaching commitment. In the process I discovered a valuable tool for dealing with personal anxieties. I learned that I could achieve peace of mind necessary to do my daily work by getting in touch with my anxieties and letting them flow out into my journal. At this point my journal entries had nothing to do with relating my life to the Lord; they were simply a means to process my anxieties so I could do my work. But the journal did fulfill a very important need in my life.

The next entry in my journal is September 1973, a full year after I began university teaching. I had totally dropped the practice of keeping a journal. This was strange. I experienced a very difficult period when I began full-time college teaching. It never occurred to me to deal with my anxieties the same way I had when writing the dissertation. For some reason in September 1973 I began recording in a journal. But I did this sporadically, only about twice a month. Occasionally my anxieties would build to a point that overwhelmed me; I would then begin recording them in the journal much the same way I had done while working on the dissertation. Most of the entries were negative. However a few positive entries began making it into the journal, such as gratitude for the success of a particular course I was teaching or gratitude for some fulfilling experiences of friendship. But the journal was still crisis centered. As yet I was making no effort to use it systematically to integrate my life more fully with the movements of the Holy Spirit. It did, however, continue to fulfill the need of relieving pressure so I could perform my daily tasks more peacefully.

After two years of teaching at the university I was asked to make tertianship, the final period of spiritual formation for Jesuit training. I chose to make tertianship during the summers of 1974 and 1975. The goal of tertianship is to allow the Jesuit time to integrate more fully Ignatian ideals with his current apostolate. I was experiencing great anxieties at the university; I decided that I could not continue in the university apostolate unless I found a way to work with more personal peace. In June 1974 I got my journal out, and, for the first time, I began to use it systematically to review all the aspects of my life, examining them to see where I was and was not responding to the Holy Spirit. I received much insight into myself and my moods during the first summer of tertianship. I returned to the university in the fall and began using my journal to apply these insights to my daily life. I jotted in my journal about three times a week, applying my summer insights to the areas in which I was now experiencing the most anxiety. I lived the year with a far greater peace than I had lived my first two years at the university. I returned for a second summer of tertianship in June 1975. Again I jotted in my journal several times a day, systematically reviewing every aspect of my life from the previous year. The recordings from the previous academic year were crucial in giving a greater insight into how I had handled my moods. I became much more aware at this time of the situations in which I habitually responded to the Spirit and those in which I did not. I left that summer of tertianship with great peace. That fall, 1975, I began recording in my journal daily, systematically reviewing my life in terms of my response to the Spirit. Since that time the journal has been for me the most important daily spiritual activity.

As I reflect back on my non-use of the journal during the years preceding tertianship, I can see that I did not make time for daily recordings because I was very busy and needed the time for my many duties and did not see clearly how the journal could help. During the tertianship, however, I had an immense amount of time on my hands; I was, in fact, often looking for ways to fill up this time. I got into the habit of recording in the journal during the first summer of tertianship, kept it up during the ensuing year and also continued recording the following summer. During this time I progressively discovered the great value the journal had for dealing with my anxieties: I discovered that my life was becoming more happy and peaceful. This new peacefulness fully justified the time spent recording. Through the systematic use of the journal I was finally recognizing and dealing effectively with my main obstacles to the Spirit, not allowing myself to be caught in bad moods that had caused so much anxiety the previous years. By the fall of 1975 I had learned the importance of daily jotting in the journal to orientate my life for the coming day as well as the importance of regularly reviewing the journal to detect patterns of non-response to the Holy Spirit. From this time to the present, my method for recording and reviewing my spiritual journal has remained rather constant.

## Method for Recording

The manner in which entries are made in the journal is crucial to the success of the journal. It must be stressed that the purpose of the journal is not to gain personal insights into our life by our own efforts; the purpose of the journal is to allow the Spirit to guide our insights. This means that we must set conditions for recording in our journal that will evoke the Spirit and allow the Spirit to affect our entry. The conditions for keeping the spiritual journal under the influence of the Holy Spirit are the same as those for making a consciousness examen under the influence of the Holy Spirit. They include an appropriate time, place, and method.

The journal should be kept at a time of day when we are most alert, quiet and capable of coming in tune with our deepest self. This time will differ for individuals. For me it is early in the morning after I get up and before I have breakfast. For the past ten years I have found the following practice most helpful. After getting up, taking a shower and shaving I relax comfortably in my prayer chair, sipping a cup of coffee for a few minutes and pausing to allow my inner moods to emerge. I then begin recording in the journal the mood or situation that is uppermost in my consciousness. The morning time is important to me for many reasons. First, it is my best time, the time I am most alert, peaceful and capable of coming into contact with my deepest self. Second, it is the only time of day I can be sure I will not be disturbed. As I move into my day, I become ever more available to others and progressively more preoccupied with the concerns of the day. Should I decide to keep my journal at noon or in the evening, I would have the double concern of quieting my mind from the activities of the day and fear of being interrupted by others.

There are two other advantages for me in keeping the journal in the morning. First, it orients me for the coming day. In the morning I can look back on the previous day and reflect on the moods of that day seeing whether or not I responded to the Spirit. Since I am usually too tired to make an extended consciousness examen at night, this morning time is my first chance to reflect on these moods. If I have anxieties that have carried over from the previous day, I can process them at this time. Also during the morning time after awakening I am in touch with the dreams from the night before. Should they have caused anxiety I can deal with this anxiety. I am just now learning the technique for using dreams well to guide my life; I see this as an important direction for myself to develop. I also look ahead to the coming day to see whether there are problems I will face that are likely to cause bad moods. I then prepare myself to deal with these problems. During this morning time my attempt is to process all my anxieties so I do not leave my room dominated by them, allowing them to be barriers to living in tune with the Spirit during the coming day.

Second, keeping the journal in the morning before my daily prayer clears my mind for prayer and often provides the content for my prayer. When I am disturbed by anxious thoughts, I am not quiet enough to pray well; this forces me to spend my prayer time examining the causes of my anxiety. If, however, I do this before prayer in my journal, my mind is quiet and ready for prayer. The particular anxiety may even provide the starting point for prayer, and I go to the Lord for healing and strength. In addition, recording my blessings in the journal before my prayer also provides content for much of my prayer. As I record these blessings, I may be moved by how greatly I have been blessed. I may then choose to rest in the Lord, grateful for my many blessings. In short the early morning time before I begin my day has proved to be the best time for me both because it removes obstacles that could affect my service during the coming day and also because it clears my mind for prayer and often provides the content for my prayer. I generally leave my room after journal-keeping and personal prayer ready to serve the Lord and others in peace.

Perhaps a note should be added on the difference between journal-keeping and prayer. To be done successfully both must be done in tune with the Holy Spirit, but their purposes do differ. The purpose of keeping the journal is to allow the Spirit to reveal to us where we are responding to the Spirit and where we are not; it is primarily self-knowledge. The purpose of prayer, however, is different. In prayer our primary goal is communion with the Lord and not self-knowledge, though that may also occur. Examination and prayer are both essential for a deep Christian life. Since many people identify prayer simply with reflection on their lives in the presence of God, it is important to clarify the distinction between the two activities. I have learned that I can be more open before God in prayer, allowing God to touch me and produce communion in any way the Spirit leads after I have completed journaling.

A second condition for keeping the journal effectively is finding a place where we will not be disturbed nor fear being disturbed. Such a place is crucial for centering. As we situate ourselves in this place at this time, we almost automatically find ourself going to the center of our being. As we begin writing in the journal, we become more in tune with our deepest self. Consequently our writing is done more and more under the guidance of the Spirit, even though we do not consciously reflect on this. I often find myself writing feelings and insights that I had not previously reflected upon but which guide me to a deeper self-understanding. It is important to be undisturbed so that this flow can continue. Some days I may write for five minutes; other days I may write for forty-five—the quiet is essential for the process to continue. So is the regularity of time and place: in this place at this time I am in an atmosphere that facilitates union with my deepest self—the place where God's Spirit touches and transforms my spirit. I should note that I journal in the same chair in which I pray. I relax and sip coffee while I'm journaling; for prayer I put the coffee aside and sit more upright and reverently. I keep my journal on a side table, right under the Bible, so I am ready both to journal and to pray each morning. I have found the $8^1/2''$ x $11''$, thin-lined spiral notebook to work best for me for journal-keeping.

I have several observations regarding my method for recording that help me to keep the journal effectively. First, I must not be rushed. I pause a minute or two before writing anything, sipping my coffee; then I begin to write. As I write I begin to feel more and more peaceful before the Lord. I am getting more in tune with my center and the Spirit is progressively emerging and affecting my recording. Indeed the recording itself often helps me to pay more attention to what is going on in my deepest self. Second, I feel no compulsion to record everything that happened the previous day. I record only those things that seem significant at the moment—the events that are responsible for my current mood, be it good or bad. Sometimes recording in the journal will even pre-empt my prayer period. It seems more important to me to come to a personal peace through my recording than it does to stop the process and begin to pray. Third, I do not censor my recordings; I write my moods, especially my bad moods, as I experience them. Initially I do not relate them to the

Spirit; I just try to get on paper what is bothering me and what is making me happy. Eventually as I write I become more and more aware of the Spirit's presence or absence in these events and may consciously relate them to the Spirit. I note that my journal does not contain a lot of explicit religious language. It is obvious to me when I reread my journal where God is and is not present in my experiences. I can record my bad moods uncensored because my journal is written only for myself. I am careful not to mention names of others if I feel this could be compromising to them. I am also careful not to be explicit about events in my life if I may find those compromising later. I have asked a friend to destroy my journals if anything should ever happen to me. Over the fifteen years I have been keeping a journal, I have never had the problem of people prying into it.

Many people tell me that they find it difficult regularly to keep a journal. I am sure that much of this is related to temperament, but I believe also that the difficulty may stem partially from the method of recording. If the proper conditions are not present, the journal can become compulsive, self-centered introspection. Too much time spent in this mode of journaling can indeed seem like "navel gazing" and not worth the time and effort. However if the conditions are present to facilitate the emergence of the Spirit, an entirely different experience is had. Being freed from the anxiety caused by bad moods is a recreating experience. Further, at times great insights come, redirecting activities and producing exhilaration carrying over into the day. Finally, it is always comforting to record the experiences of the previous day and to realize that the Lord's presence has been woven through them—frequently I do not fully appreciate the presence of the Lord in my day until I begin writing in my journal. Only then can the full sense of gratitude emerge. In short I do not experience the time spent recording in the journal as an odious and futile chore that I impose upon myself, but rather as a freeing and refreshing activity producing a deeper union with God during the recording itself as well as during the upcoming day.

### Content: Tracing the Spirit

The content of my journal is, of course, highly personal, reflecting my life situation and my particular temperament. This is important to keep in mind; I do not intend to suggest that every spiritual journal will be similar to mine in content and in tone. It is difficult to isolate all the different types of entries in my journal. I believe that the following five threads do occur most frequently: processing and handling my bad moods, recording my blessings, reflecting on the progress of my work, planning new service, and, finally, general observations on life and theological musings.

The greatest amount of space in my journal is concerned with processing and handling my bad moods. The journal is my primary tool for recognizing when I am responding to the Spirit and when I am not. These moods arise in the morning from recollection of situations of the previous day, from anticipation of problems of the coming day and from restless sleep with unsettling dreams. If I am experiencing a bad mood, it will emerge in my process of quieting down and preparing to write in my journal. I then begin recording the mood with all the factors surrounding it, attempting to understand its causes. At this point I do not attempt to relate it to the presence or absence of the Holy Spirit. Often as I write the mood in some detail, it dissipates and a new peace emerges. This is especially true if the mood has been produced by internal anxieties I have created rather than from an objective situation in my life. If the mood does not dissipate during the recording and is still dominating my feelings, I will take the troublesome situation as my particular examen for the coming day.

I have found it helpful for myself to begin each morning entry with an indication of my mood the previous day and at the present moment. I record two numbers using a scale of 0–5; 0 represents total lack of sensible consolation and 5 represents the highest degree of consolation. The first number indicates the mood of the previous day; the second the present mood. My commonest entry is 3: this means that I am experiencing myself as living in tune with the Spirit because I have been living in peace and with the desire to love and serve others in my daily duties. The numbers are most helpful for me in reviewing my journal. At a glance I can pick out those entries that are lower than 3. By putting these entries alongside of each other in my mind, I can review them to see if there are patterns of anxieties that have arisen in my life over the previous period. If there have been patterns, I can then plan a method for dealing with the causes of these anxieties. Since I review my journal weekly, monthly and annually, these numbers are quick reference points for me and helpful for that reason. It is also heartening to note the numbers above 3; these are usually indications that I have been experiencing greater than ordinary blessings. It is bracing for me to recall them both in order to give God appropriate thanks and in order to put my life in perspective if I am currently dominated by bad moods. My life is very busy and I tend to lose touch with these blessings.

The next most common entry in my journal is the recording of my blessings. Often as I quiet down in the morning, I am moved by the richness of my previous day and so begin writing all those things that brought me fulfillment. They are usually related to success in some work I am doing or to growth in relationships to students and other friends. It often surprises me how recording one blessing triggers my awareness of others. There are days when the only recordings I make are blessings; indeed, in recent times the blessings have occupied more space than the bad moods and anxieties—quite a contrast to earlier recordings! I should note again that I do not initially relate these to the Spirit. The process of recording them, however, does make me more aware of how completely my life the previous day has been touched by the Spirit. My journal reflects that there are periods in my life that are dominated by the awareness of blessings and periods that are dominated by preoccupation with problems and anxieties. I record what emerges in my consciousness as I become quiet, whether these be blessings or anxieties. I have no preconceived format about what ought to be included in a particular journal entry. Nor do I begin my recording by asking the question: "Where was the Spirit present and absent in my day?" As I record both my good moods and my bad moods, this becomes all too clear.

A third very common entry in my journal is the reflection on the progress of my work. I like to review what I have done the previous day and record what has gone well or poorly. If my work has gone well, this may have emerged as a blessing in a previous entry; likewise if my work has gone poorly, it may have already emerged as an anxiety in my journal. If my work has been frustrating, I will attempt to get to the cause of the frustration. I then plan ahead to see how I can remove the frustration and perform my work more effectively. My chief work is teaching. I frequently reflect on the progress of a course to see if it is necessary to add a dimension to it or to remove something that really is not working well. I leave my reflection only when I am positively orientated to the work I must do the coming day and have corrected the problems with the work flowing from the previous day.

I also use my journal to plan future service for the kingdom. I regularly receive requests for special presentations and series. I have found it is best not to respond immediately. I bring the requests to my journal for reflection. Often I use the method I have described in Chapter 4 for finding God's will regarding a particular request. I note reasons for and against the request over a period of days, returning to these lists during these days to see whether or not my mind, will and feelings are orienting toward or away from the decision. I will also do long-range planning for my life. For instance several years ago I had a book published. The idea of writing a book on spirituality occurred to me over ten years ago. At that time, however, it was not clear to me exactly how many chapters should be in the book or what the content of these chapters should be. Using my journal the number of chapters and the content of the chapters gradually evolved. Some of the chapters were published as articles before the book appeared. During a recent review of my old journals I was able to trace the evolution of this book. I could observe in the journal the origin of my desire to write a book, the emergence of the content of the individual chapters, and gradually the emergence of a total view of the book. I often get a sense of how Providence is working in my life as I review my journal.

The fifth type of entry resists easy categorization. As I begin writing, I may just want to delve into relationships I am experiencing with a friend, trying to understand better the dynamics of what is happening between us. I also enjoy recording my observations on life, both regarding my immediate living situation and regarding world events. I ruminate on the situations, attempting to understand them better. In addition to these musings I often find myself speculating on theological questions that touch my professional work. I enjoy recording new insights into the theological questions that are currently occupying me. I am able to trace the development of my understanding of a particular theological topic in the entries of my journal.

The primary purpose of my journal is to reflect on my life in terms of how well or poorly I am responding to the Holy Spirit in my daily activity. To accomplish this most effectively, however, I must stress that it is important that I record my daily moods, good as well as bad, just as I experience them, without any attempt to relate them immediately to the Spirit. An over-concern with seeing whether the Spirit is or is not present in a mood may short-circuit the full emergence of what is welling up from the center of my being. My goal is to get in touch with these moods. Recording these moods as I experience them becomes the raw material for all subsequent reflections on my life. If these moods truly reflect what is going on deep inside of me, then I will have an accurate "handle" for dealing with them. Only after I have recorded them can I stand back and observe where the Spirit has been present and absent and then guide my life accordingly.

### Reviewing the Spiritual Journal

The above reflections have focused upon the role of the journal in preparing me to serve better during the coming day. But over the years I have observed an increasing pattern of reviewing these daily jottings. I review my journal weekly, monthly and yearly. These reviews give me a larger perspective on my life, enabling me to see the patterns of activity in which God is present and not present. I often find myself unreflectively responding to all the demands made upon me but without a quality of heart that flows from the presence of the Spirit. I do not see this clearly until I look back over a period. These periodic reviews give me the opportunity to catch myself and reorientate myself.

Since I have more free time on weekends than I do during the week, I use Saturday or Sunday morning as an opportunity for reviewing weekly and monthly entries. During these times I make extended entries in my journal. This for me has taken the place of the traditional day of recollection. I have evolved the following process. First I quietly read the entries for the previous period, usually while sitting in my prayer chair and sipping a cup of coffee. Then on a single page of my journal I make two columns, one entitled Blessings, the other Obstacles. Under the appropriate column I record all the major blessings and obstacles I have noted in my journal when reflecting on the entries from that period. I am especially attentive to the obstacle list. I evaluate the list to see if a pattern of non-response to the Spirit has emerged. If one has, I reflect on it to understand its causes and its pervasiveness in my life. I then record means for dealing with this pattern. Frequently this means adopting a particular examen to better handle the troublesome situation in the coming days. The review process may take an hour. I often set aside time later in the day to take a long walk, reflecting on my review and reorientating myself accordingly. I summarize my conclusion the following day in my journal. In addition to reflecting on the entries from the previous period, I also review the entries made during my annual retreat to see whether or not I am living out the ideals and resolutions I made then. During my annual retreat, I should note, I make extended entries each day. At the end of the retreat I summarize the insights of the retreat and then use those as a guide for my life during the coming year.

In addition to these weekly and monthly reviews, I also review my journal during my annual eight-day retreat. I leisurely read through the entire year at several sittings, paying special attention to blessings, obstacles to the Spirit and fulfillment of my previous retreat resolutions. I do this during the opening days of the retreat, jotting down anything significant that appears. Again I will make two lists, the first for blessings, the second for obstacles. Getting in contact with my daily patterns from the previous year is crucial for the success of my annual retreat. These patterns are the starting points for my gratitude toward God as well as for the redirection of my life. Without the data of the journal I would have very little idea of the general patterns or the significant occurrences of my life during the previous year. During the retreat I make several entries a day in the journal. Before the retreat ends, I pull together the decisions I wish to implement during the coming year: I articulate the particular image of Christ I hope to follow; I list resolutions to be implemented during my daily spiritual life; I list particular new services I feel called to undertake for the greater glory of God. I will refer to these lists during the periodic reviews of my journal in the coming year.

I should note that the review of my journal is not an odious obligation I impose on myself. I continue these reviews because they always bring me great insight and peace. Frankly they are usually prompted by an increasing anxiety I observe in myself. The review gives me the opportunity to reflect on this anxiety, to get back on course if I have gone off and to re-establish myself in the peace that flows from living in response to the Spirit. These reviews have become my primary mode of spiritual direction. They are also helpful in presenting myself more completely to my bi-weekly spiritual direction group and to my spiritual director. I have noted, however, that the frequency of my need for seeing a spiritual director has dwindled dramatically as I became more faithful to doing reflection on my own life through my spiritual journal.

## Freedom in the Spirit

The goal of our life is to love God and others with our whole heart, soul, mind and body. As we move closer each day toward the realization of this ideal, we find ourselves becoming more free and more loving. We are becoming what we have been created by the Lord to be—children of God led by the Spirit of God. And we are experiencing the freedom that comes only from living in tune with the Spirit: "Now this Lord is the Spirit, and where the Spirit of the Lord is, there is freedom" (2 Cor 3:17). We are more free because we are no longer slaves of forces that block our response to God's presence, and we are more loving because we have become ever more responsive to the Spirit of love in the ordinary activities of each day. In short we are becoming contemplatives in action! But this acknowledgement prompts no pride—only humility. We know the ultimate source of our holiness: God's Spirit in our heart. With gratitude we join with Mary in praying our own magnificat to the Lord: "My soul magnifies the Lord, and my spirit rejoices in God my Savior because he who is mighty has done great things for me and holy is his name."

## REFLECTION QUESTIONS

1. If you have stopped keeping a journal after having kept one, explain why you stopped. Does anything from this chapter suggest how your previous practice could have been more effective for your spiritual life?

2. If you are presently keeping a journal, how does it relate to implementing your Christian life goals?

3. If you have kept or are keeping a journal, compare and contrast your method for recording in the journal with the method presented here.

4. If you are keeping or have kept a journal, compare and contrast the contents of your entries with the content of the entries described in the chapter.

5. If you are keeping or have kept a journal, compare and contrast your reviewing of your journal entries with the review methods presented here.

6. If you do not keep a journal, discuss the reasons why you don't. After reading this chapter, do you see any way in which some type of spiritual journal could be helpful for your Christian living?

# NOTES

## Introduction

1. Richard J. Hauser, S.J., *In His Spirit: A Guide to Today's Spirituality* (New York: Paulist Press, 1982).

2. Louis J. Puhl, S.J., *The Spiritual Exercises of St. Ignatius: Based on Studies in the Language of the Autograph* (Chicago: Loyola University Press, 1951).

3. The writings of these Jesuits that have directly contributed to my understanding of Ignatian thought are listed in the Selected Bibliography.

4. Jules A. Toner, S.J., *A Commentary on Saint Ignatius' Rules for the Discernment of Spirits: A Guide to the Principles and Practice* (St. Louis: The Institute of Jesuit Sources, 1982). This book deserves special mention. It was the text of Fr. Toner's course. It is the definitive study on Ignatius' Rules for Discernment of Spirits. Only after I had read and grasped it did I feel confident enough to write the present book.

## Chapter I: Awakening to the Holy Spirit

1. All Scripture quotations are taken from *The Jerusalem Bible,* except where indicated otherwise. In my own text I have avoided using the pronouns *he* or *she* for *God.* I have, however, used the appellation *Father,* respecting the text of *The Jerusalem Bible,* the traditional usage in the Lord's Prayer and Jesus' own usage.

2. The book I have found most helpful in understanding the spiritual path is Evelyn Underhill's classic *Mysticism.*

## Chapter II: Recognizing the Holy Spirit

1. Quotation taken from J. Patout Burns, S.J. and Gerald M. Fagin, S.J., *The Holy Spirit: Message of the Fathers of the Church, Volume 3* (Wilmington, DE: Michael Glazier, Inc., 1984), p. 182.

2. Chapter V of my book *In His Spirit: A Guide to Today's Spirituality* deals at length with these principles of asceticism.

## Chapter III: Obstacles to the Spirit

1. George Aschenbrenner, S.J. wrote an article that has influenced greatly my understanding of the consciousness examen. It appeared in *Review for Religious*, Vol 31, No. 1, 1972, pp. 14–21. The method I am presenting for the examen is similar to but not identical with his method.

## Chapter IV: Seeking God's Will

1. My thinking on this topic was influenced greatly by Jules Toner, S.J. in a course I took from him on Ignatian Discernment in the summer of 1983. Fr. Toner is currently preparing a book on the method Ignatius presents in *The Spiritual Exercises* for finding God's will. Though my thinking has been influenced greatly by Fr. Toner, my approach is definitely not identical with his.

2. Avery Dulles, S.J. wrote an article called "Finding God's Will" that has helped me organize my thinking. It appeared in *Woodstock Letters*, Spring 1965, pp. 139–152. The article is a reflection upon a scholarly treatise by Karl Rahner, "The Logic of Concrete Individual Knowledge in Ignatius Loyola," in *The Dynamic Element in the Church* (trans. W.J. O'Hara; *Quaestiones Disputatae 12;* New York: Herder & Herder, 1964), pp. 84–170.

3. Frs. Avery Dulles and Karl Rahner are among these theologians.

## Chapter V: Keeping a Spiritual Journal

1. A version of this chapter entitled "Keeping a Spiritual Journal: Personal Reflections" appeared in *Review for Religious*, Vol. 42, No.

4, 1983, pp. 575–584. I am grateful to the *Review* for permission to use it here.

2. Ira Progoff has written two books describing these workshops: *At a Journal Workshop* and *The Practice of Process Meditation.* Both are available from Dialogue House Library, 80 East 11th Street, New York, NY 10003. The books can be used more effectively after having experienced the workshop itself.

# SELECTED BIBLIOGRAPHY

I have listed in alphabetical order only those authors and their publications that have directly influenced my own approach. Some have already appeared in the Notes.

Aschenbrenner, George A., S.J. "Consciousness Examen," *Review for Religious,* Vol. 31, No. 1, 1972, pp. 14–21.

Asselin, David T., S.J. "Christian Maturity and Spiritual Discernment", *Review for Religious,* Vol. 27, 1968, pp. 581–595.

Buckley, Michael, S.J. "Rules for the Discernment of Spirits," *The Way Supplement 20,* Autumn 1973, pp. 19–37.

Dulles, Avery, S.J. "Finding God's Will," *Woodstock Letters,* Spring 1965, pp. 139–152.

English, John, S.J. "Discernment and the Examen," from taped conferences in London, Ontario, March 7, 1973.

Futrell, John, S.J. "Communal Discernment: Reflections on Experience," *Studies in the Spirituality of Jesuits,* Vol. 4, No. 5, Nov. 1972, pp. 159–194.

Futrell, John, S.J. "Ignatian Discernment," *Studies in the Spirituality of Jesuits,* Vol. 2, No. 2, April 1970, pp. 47–88.

Green, Thomas, S.J. *Weeds Among the Wheat: Discernment: Where Prayer and Action Meet* (Notre Dame: Ave Maria Press, 1984).

Hauser, Richard, S.J. *In His Spirit: A Guide to Today's Spirituality* (New York: Paulist Press, 1982).

Puhl, Louis, S.J. *The Spiritual Exercises of St. Ignatius: Based on Studies in the Language of the Autograph* (Chicago: Loyola University Press, 1951).

Rahner, Karl. *The Dynamic Element in the Church* (New York: Herder and Herder, 1964).

Toner, Jules, S.J. *A Commentary on Saint Ignatius' Rules for the Discernment of Spirits: A Guide to the Principles and Practice.* (St. Louis: The Institute of Jesuit Sources, 1982).

Toner, Jules, S.J. "The Deliberation That Started the Jesuits," *Studies in the Spirituality of Jesuits,* Vol. 6, No. 4, June 1974, pp. 179–216.

Toner, Jules, S.J. "A Method for Communal Discernment of God's Will," *Studies in the Spirituality of Jesuits,* Vol. 3, No. 4, Sept. 1971, pp. 121–152.

Underhill, Evelyn. *Mysticism: A Study in the Nature and Development of Man's Spiritual Consciousness* (New York: The New American Library, Inc., 1955).

Young, William, S.J. (trans.). *St. Ignatius' Own Story* (As told to Luis Gonzalez de Camara) (Chicago: Loyola University Press, 1980).